Mahomet I

By Gladys M. Draycott

INTRODUCTION

The impetus that gave victory to Islam is spent. Since its material prosperity overwhelmed its spiritual ascendancy in the first years of triumph its vitality has waned under the stress of riches, then beneath lassitude and the slow decrease of power. The Prophet Mahomet is at once the glory and bane of his people, the source of their strength and the mainspring of their weakness. He represents more effectively than any other religious teacher the sum of his followers' spiritual and worldly ideas. His position in religion and philosophy is substantially the position of all his followers; none have progressed beyond the primary thesis he gave to the Arabian world at the close of his career.

He closes a long line of semi-divine teachers and monitors. After him the curtains of heaven close, and its glory is veiled from men's eyes. He is the last great man who imposed enthusiasm for an idea upon countless numbers of his fellow-creatures, so that whole tribes fought and died at his bidding, and at the command of God through him. Now that the vital history of Islam has been written, some decision as to the position and achievements of its founder may be formulated.

Mahomet conceived the office of Prophet to be the result of an irresistible divine call. Verily the angel Gabriel appeared to him, commanding him to "arise and warn." He was the vehicle through whom the will of Allah was revealed. The inspired character of his rule was the prime factor in its prevailing; by virtue of his heavenly authority he exercised his sway over the religious actions of his followers, their aspirations and their beliefs. In order to promulgate the divine ordinances the Kuran was sent down, inspired directly by the angel Gabriel at the bidding of the Lord. Upon all matters of belief and upon all other matters dealt with, however cursorily, in the Kuran Mahomet spoke with the power of God Himself; upon matters not within the scope of religion or of the Sacred Book he was only a human and fallible counsellor.

"I am no more than man; when I order you anything with respect to religion, receive it, and when I order you about the affairs of the world, then am I nothing more than man."

There is no question of his equality with the Godhead, or even of his sharing any part of the divine nature. He is simply the instrument, endowed with a power and authority outside himself, a man who possesses one cardinal thesis which all those within his faith must accept.

The idea which represents at once the scope of his teaching and the source of his triumphs is the unity and indivisibility of the Godhead. This is the sole contribution he has made to the progressive thought of the world. Though he came later in time than the culture of Greece and Rome, he never knew their philosophies or the sum of their knowledge. His religion could never he built upon such basic strength as Christianity. It sprang too rapidly into prominence, and had no foundation of slowly developed ideas upon which to rest both its enthusiasm and its earthly endeavour.

Mahomet bears closer resemblance to the ancient Hebrew prophets than to any Christian leader or saint. His mind was akin to theirs in its denunciatory fury, its prostration before the might and majesty of a single God. The evolution of the tribal deity from the local wonderworker, whose shrine enclosed his image, to the impersonal and distant but awful power who held the earth beneath his sway, was Mahomet's contribution to the mental development of his country, and the achievement within those confines was wonderful. But to the sum of the world's thought he gave little. His central tenet had already gained its votaries in other lands, and, moreover, their form of belief in one God was such that further development of thought was still possible to them. The philosophy of Islam blocks the way of evolution for itself, because its system leaves no room for such pregnant ideas as divine incarnation, divine immanence, the fatherhood of God. It has been content to formulate one article of faith: "There is no God but God," the corollary as to Mahomet's divine appointment to the office of Prophet being merely an affirmation of loyalty to the particular mode of faith he imposed. Therefore the part taken by Islam in the reading of the world's mystery ceased with the acceptance of that previously conceived central tenet.

In the sphere of ideas, indeed, Mahomet gave his people nothing original, for his power did not lie in intellect, but in action. His mind had not passed the stage that has just exchanged many fetishes for one spiritual God, still to be propitiated, not alone by sacrifices, but by prayers, ceremonies, and praise. In the world of action lay the strength of Islam and the genius of its founder; it is therefore in the impress it made upon events and not in its theology and philosophy that its secret is to be found. But besides the acceptance of one God as Lord, Islam forced upon its devotees a still more potent idea, whose influence is felt both in the spheres of thought and action.

As an outcome of its political and military needs Mahomet created and established its unassailable belief in fatality—not the fatalism of cause and effect, bearing within itself the essence of a reason too vast for humanity to comprehend, but the fatalism of an omnipotent and capricious power inherent in the Mahomedan conception of God. With this mighty and irresponsible being nothing can prevail. Before every event the result of it is irrevocably decreed. Mankind can alter no tiniest detail of his destined lot. The idea corresponds with Mahomet's vision of God—an awful, incomprehensible deity, who dwells perpetually in the terrors of earth, not in its gentleness and compassion. The doctrine of fatalism proved Islam's greatest asset during its first hard years of struggle, for it gave to its battlefields the glory of God's surveillance: "Death is a favour to a Muslim." But with prosperity and conquest came inaction; then fatalism, out of the weakening of endurance, created the pessimism of Islam's later years. Being philosophically uncreative, it descended into the sloth of those who believe, without exercise of reason or will, in the uselessness of effort.

Before Islam decayed into inertia it had experienced a fierce and flaming life. The impulse bestowed upon it by its founder operated chiefly in the religious world, and indirectly in the realm of political and military power. How far the religion of Islam is indebted to Mahomet's knowledge of the Jewish and Christian systems becomes clear upon a study of the Kuran and the Muslim institutions. That Mahomet was familiar with Jewish Scriptures and tradition is beyond doubt.

The middle portion of the Kuran is filled to the point of weariness with reiterations of Jewish legend and hero-myths. It is evident that Mahomet took the God of the Jews to be his own deity, combining in his conception also the traditional connection of Jehovah and His Chosen People with the ancient faith and ceremonies of Mecca, purged of their idolatries. From the Jews he took his belief in the might and terror of the Lord and the admonitory character of his mission. From them also he took the separatist nature of his creed. The Jewish teachers postulated a religion distinct from every other belief, self-sufficient, owning no interpreter save the Law and the Scriptures. Mahomet conceived himself also as the sole vehicle during his lifetime and after his death for the commands of the Most High. He aimed at the superseding of Rabbinical power, and hoped to win the Jews into recognition of himself as successor to their own teachers and prophets.

But his claims were met by an unyielding reliance upon the completed Law. If the Jewish religion had rejected a Redeemer from among its own people, it was impossible that it should accept a leader from an alien and despised race. Mahomet, finding coalition impossible, gave free play to his separatist instinct, so that in this respect, and also in its fundamental conception of the deity, as well as in its reliance upon inspired Scriptures and oral traditions, Mahomedanism approximates to the Jewish system. It misses the influence of an immemorial history, and receives no help in its campaign of warfare from the traditional glories of long lines of warrior kings. Chief of all, it lacks the inspiration of the matchless Jewish Scriptures and Sacred Books, depending for instruction upon a document confined to the revelation of one man's personality and view of life.

Still the narrowness of the Mahomedan system provoked its power; its rapid rush to the heights Of dominion was born of the straitening of its impulse into the channel of conquest and the forcible imposition of its faith.

Of Christianity Mahomet knew far less than of Judaism. He went to the Christian doctrines as they were known in heterodox Syria, far off from the main stream of Christian life and teaching. He went to them with a prejudiced mind, full of anger against their exponents for declaring the Messiah to be the Son of God. The whole idea of the Incarnation and the dogma of the Trinity were thoroughly abhorrent to him, and the only conception he entertains as to the personality of Jesus is that of a Prophet even as he is himself, the receiver of divine inspiration, but having no connection in essence with God, whom he conceived pre-eminently as the one supreme Being, indivisible in nature. Certainly he knew far less of the Christian than of the Jewish Scriptures, and necessarily less of the inner meaning of the Christian faith, still in fluid state, unconsidered of its profoundest future exponents. His mind was assuredly not attuned to the reception of its more revolutionary ideas. Very little compassion and no tenderness breathe from the pages of the Kuran, and from a religion whose Founder had laboured to bring just those two elements into the thorny ways of the world, Mahomet could only turn away baffled and uncomprehending. The doctrine of the non-resistance to evil, and indeed all the wisdom of the Sermon on the Mount, he passed by unseeing.

It is useless and indeed unfair to attempt the comparison of Mahomedanism with Christianity, seeing that without the preliminary culture of Greece and Rome modern Christian doctrines would not exist in their present form, and of the former Mahomet had no cognisance. He stands altogether apart from the Christian system, finding no affinity in its doctrines or practices, scorning its monasticism no less than its conception of the Trinity. His position in history lies between the warriors and the saints, at the head of the Prophets, who went, flail in hand, to summon to repentance, but unlike the generality, bearing also the sword and sceptre of a kingdom.

No other religious leader has ever bound his creed so closely to definite political conceptions, Mahomet was not only the instrument of divine revelation, but he was also at the end of his life the head of a temporal state with minutest laws and regulations—chaotic it may be, but still binding so that Islamic influence extended over the whole of the lives of its adherents. This constitutes its strength. Its leader swayed not only the convictions but the activities of his subjects.

His position with regard to the political institution of other countries is unique. His temporal power grew almost in spite of himself, and he unconsciously adopted ideas in connection with it which arose out of the circumstances involved. Any form of government except despotism was impossible among so heterogeneous and unruly a people; despotism also bore out his own idea as to the nature of God's governance. Political ideas were largely built upon religious conceptions, sometimes outstripping, sometimes lagging behind them, but always with some irrefragable connection. Despotism, therefore, was the form best suited to Islam, and becomes its chief legacy to posterity, since without the religious sanction Islam politically could not exist.

Together with despotism and inextricably mingled with it is the second great Islamic enthusiasm—the belief in the supremacy of force. With violence the Muslim kingdom was to be attained. Mahomet gave to the battle lust of Arabia the approval of his puissant deity, bidding his followers put their supreme faith in the arbitrament of the sword. He knew, too, the value of diplomacy and the use of well-calculated treachery, but chief of all he bade his followers arm themselves to seize by force what they could not obtain by cunning. In the insistence upon these two factors, complete obedience to his will as the revelation of Allah's decrees and the justification of violence to proclaim the merits of his faith, we gain the nearest approach to his character and beliefs; for these, together with his conception of fate, are perhaps the most personal of all his institutions.

Mahomet has suffered not a little at the hands of his immediate successors. They have sought to record the full sum of his personality, and finding the subject elude them, as the translation of actions into words must ever fall short of finality, they have overloaded their narrative with minutest and almost always apocryphal details which leave the main outlines blurred. Only two biographies can be said to be in the nature of sources, that of Muhammad ibn Hischam, written on the model of an earlier biography, undertaken about 760 for the Abbasside Caliph Mansur, and of Wakidi, written about 820, which is important as containing the text of many treaties made by Mahomet with various tribes. Al-Tabari, too, included the life of Mahomet in his extensive history of Arabia, but his work serves only as a check, consisting, as it does, mainly of extracts from Wakidi. By far the more valuable is the Kuran and the Sunna of tradition. But even these are fragmentary and confused, bearing upon them the ineradicable stamp of alien writers and much second-hand thought.

In the dim, pregnant dawn of religions, by the transfusing power of a great idea, seized upon and made living by a single personality, the world of imagination mingles with the world of fact as we perceive it. The real is felt to be merely the frail shell of forces more powerful and permanent. Legend and myth crowd in upon actual life as imperfect vehicles for the compelling demand made by that new idea for expression. Moreover, personality, that subtle essence, exercises a kind of centripetal force, attracting not only the devotion but the imaginations of those who come within its influence.

Mahomet, together with all the men of action in history, possessed an energy of will so vast as to bring forth the creative faculties of his adherents, and the legends that cluster round him have a special significance as the measure of his personality and influence. The story, for instance, of his midnight journey into the seven heavens is the symbol of an intense spiritual experience that, following the mental temper of the age in which he lived, had to be translated into the concrete. All the affirmations as to his intercourse with Djinn, his inspiration by the angel Gabriel, are inherent factors in the manifestation of his ceaseless mental activity. His marvellous birth and the myths of his childhood are the sum of his followers' devotion, and reveal their reverence translated into terms of the imagination. Character was the mysterious force that his co-religionists tried unconsciously to portray in all those legends relative to his life at Medina, his ruthlessness and cruelty finding a place no less than his humility, and steadfastness under discouragement.

But beneath the weight of the marvellous the real man is almost buried. He has stood for so long with the mists of obscure imaginings about him that his true lineaments are almost impossible to reproduce. The Western world has alternated between the conception of him as a devil, almost Antichrist himself, and a negligible impostor whose power is transient. It has seldom troubled to look for the human energy that wrought out his successes, the faith that upheld them, and the enthusiasm that burned in the Prophet himself with a sombre flame, lighting his followers to prayer and conquest.

And indeed it is difficult, if not impossible, to re-create effectively the world in which he lived. It is so remote from the seas of the world's progression, an eddy in the tide of belief which loses itself in the larger surging, that it makes no appeal of familiarity. But that a study of the period and Mahomet's own personality operating no less through his deeds, faith, and institutions than in the one doubtfully reliable record of his teachings, will result in the perception of the Prophet of Islam as a man among men, has been the central belief during the writing of this biography. Mahomet's personality is revealed in his dealing with his fellows, in the belief and ritual that he imposed upon Arabia, in the mighty achievement of a political unity and military discipline, and therein he shows himself inexorable, cruel, passionate, treacherous, bad, subject to depression and overwhelming doubt, but never weak or purposeless, continually the master of his circumstances, whom no emergency found unprepared, whose confidence in himself nothing could shake, and who by virtue of enthusiasm and resistless activity wrested his triumphs from the hands of his enemies, and bequeathed to his followers his own unconquerable faith and the means wherewith they might attain wealth and sovereignty.

CHAPTER I

MAHOMET'S BIRTHPLACE

"And how many cities were mightier in strength than thy city that hath cast thee forth?"—*The Kuran.*

In Arabia nature cannot be ignored. Pastures and cornland, mountain slopes and quiet rivers may be admired, even reverenced; but they are things external to the gaze, and make no insistent demand upon the spirit for penetration of their mystery. Arabia, and Mecca as typical of Arabia, is a country governed by earth's primal forces. It has not yet emerged from the shadow of that early world, bare and chaotic, where a blinding sun pours down upon dusty mountain ridges, and nothing is temperate or subdued. It fosters a race of men, whose gods are relentless and inscrutable, revealing themselves seldom, and dwelling in a fierce splendour beyond earthly knowledge. To the spirit of a seeker for truth with senses alert to the outer world, this country speaks of boundless force, and impels into activity under the spur of conviction; by its very desolation it sets its ineradicable mark upon the creed built up within it.

Mahomet spent forty years in the city of Mecca, watching its temple services with his grandfather, taking part in its mercantile life, learning something of Christian and Jewish doctrine through the varied multitudes that thronged its public places. In the desert beyond the city boundaries he wandered, searching for inspiration, waiting dumbly in the darkness until the angel Gabriel descended with rush of wings through the brightness of heaven, commanding:

"Cry aloud, in the name of the Lord who created thee. O, thou enwrapped in thy mantle, arise and warn!"

Mecca lies in a stony valley midway between Yemen, "the Blessed," and Syria, in the midst of the western coast-chain of Arabia, which slopes gradually towards the Red Sea. The height of Abu Kobeis overlooks the eastern quarter of the town, whence hills of granite stretch to the holy places, Mina and Arafat, enclosed by the ramparts of the Jebel Kora range. Beyond these mountains to the south lies Taif, with its glory of gardens and fruit-trees. But the luxuriance of Taif finds no counterpart on the western side. Mecca is barren and treeless; its sandy stretches only broken here and there by low hills of quartz or gneiss, scrub-covered and dusty. The sun beats upon the shelterless town until it becomes a great cauldron within its amphitheatre of hills. During the Greater Pilgrimage the cauldron seethes with heat and humanity, and surges over into Mina and Arafat. In the daytime Mecca is limitless heat and noise, but under the stars it has all the magic of a dream-city in a country of wide horizons.

The shadow of its ancient prosperity, when it was the centre of the caravan trade from Yemen to Syria, still hung about it in the years immediately before the birth of Mahomet, and the legends concerning the founding of the city lingered in the native mind. Hagar, in her terrible journey through the desert, reached Mecca and laid her son in the midst of the valley to go on the hopeless quest for water. The child kicked the ground in torment, and God was merciful, so that from his heel marks arose a spring of clear water—the well Zemzem, hallowed ever after by Meccans. In this desolate place part of the Amalekites and tribes from Yemen settled; the child Ishmael grew up amongst them and founded his race by marrying a daughter of the chief. Abraham visited him, and under his guidance the native temple of the Kaaba was built and dedicated to the true God, but afterwards desecrated by the worship of idols within it.

Such are the legends surrounding the foundation of Mecca and of the Kaaba, of which, as of the legends concerning the early days of Rome, it may be said that they are chiefly interesting as throwing light upon the character of the race which produced them. In the case of Mecca they were mainly the result of an unconscious desire to associate the city as far as possible with the most renowned heroes of old time, and also to conciliate the Jewish element within Arabia, now firmly planted at Medina, Kheibar, and some of the adjoining territory, by insisting on a Jewish origin for their holy of holies, and as soon as Abraham and Ishmael were established as fathers of the race, legends concerning them were in perpetual creation.

The Kaaba thus reputed to be the work of Abraham bears evidence of an antiquity so remote that its beginnings will be forever lost to us. From very early times it was a goal of pilgrimage for all Arabia, because of the position of Mecca upon the chief trade route, and united in its ceremonies the native worship of the sun and stars, idols and misshapen stones. The Black Stone, the kissing of which formed the chief ceremonial, is a relic of the rites practised by the stone-worshippers of old; while the seven circuits of the Kaaba, obligatory on all pilgrims, are probably a symbol of the courses of the planets. Arab divinities, such as Alilat and Uzza, were associated with the Kaaba before any records are available, and at the time of Mahomet, idolatry mingled with various rites still held sway among the Meccans, though the leaven of Jewish tradition was of great help to him in the establishment of the monotheistic idea. At Mahomet's birth the Kaaba consisted of a small roofless house, with the Black Stone imbedded in its wall. Near it lay the well Zemzem, and the reputed grave of Ishmael. The Holy Place of Arabia held thus within itself traces of a purer faith, that were to be discovered and filled in by Mahomet, until the Kaaba became the goal of thousands, the recipient of the devotion and longings of that mighty host of Muslim who went forth to subdue the world. Mahomet's ancestors had for some time held a high position in the city. He came of the race of Hashim, whose privilege it was to give service to the pilgrims coming to worship at the Kaaba. The Hashim were renowned for generosity, and Mahomet's grandfather, Abd al Muttalib, was revered by the Kureisch, inhabitants of Mecca, as a just and honourable man, who had greatly increased their prosperity by his rediscovery of the holy well.

Its healing waters had been choked by the accumulations of years, so that even the knowledge of its site was lost, when an angel appeared to Abd al Muttalib, as he slept at the gate of the temple, saying:

"Dig up that which is pure!"

Three times the command fell on uncomprehending ears, until the angel revealed to the sleeper where the precious water might be found. And as he dug, the well burst forth once more, and behold within its deeps lay two golden gazelles, with weapons, the treasure of former kings. And there was strife among the Kureisch for the possession of these riches, until they were forced to draw lots. So the treasure fell to Abd al Muttalib, who melted the weapons to make a door for the Kaaba, and set up the golden gazelles within it.

Abd al Muttalib figures very prominently in the early legends concerning Mahomet, because he was sole guardian of the Prophet during very early childhood. These legends are mainly later accretions, but the kernel of truth within them is not difficult to discover. Like all forerunners of the great teachers, he stands in communion with heavenly messengers, the symbol of his purity of heart. He is humble, compassionate, and devout, living continually in the presence of his god—a fitting guardian for the renewer of the faith of his nation. Most significant of the legends is the story of his vow to sacrifice a son if ten were born to him, and of the choice of Abdullah, Mahomet's father, and the repeated staying of the father's hand, so that the sacrifice could not be accomplished until is son's life was bought with the blood of a hundred camels. This and all allied legends are fruit of a desire to magnify the divine authority of Mahomet's mission by dwelling on the intervention of a higher power in the disposal of his fate.

Of Abd al Muttalib's ten sons, Abdallah was the most handsome in form and stature, so that the fame of his beauty spread into the harems of the city, and many women coveted him in their hearts. But he, after his father had sacrificed the camels in his stead, went straightway to the house of Amina, a maiden well-born and lovely, and remained there to complete his nuptials with her. Then, after some weeks, he departed to Gaza for the exchange of merchandise, but, returning, was overtaken by sickness and died at Medina.

Amina, left thus desolate, sought the house of Abd al Muttalib, where she stayed until her child was born. Visions of his future greatness were vouchsafed to her before his birth by an angel, who told her the name he was to bear, and his destiny as Prophet of his people. Long before the child's eyes opened to the light, a brightness surrounded his mother, so that by it might be seen the far-off towers of the castles in Syrian Bostra. A tenderness hangs over the story of Mahomet's birth, akin to that immortal beauty surrounding the coming of Christ. We have faint glimpses of Amina, in the dignity of her sorrow, waiting for the birth of her son, and in the house of Mecca's leading citizen, hearing around her not alone the celestial voices of her spirit-comforters, but also rumours of earthly strife and the threatenings of strange armies from the south.

At Sana, capital of Yemen, ruled Abraha, king of the southern province. He built a vast temple within its walls, and purposed to make Sana the pilgrim-city for all Arabia. But the old custom still clove to Mecca, and finding he could in nowise coerce the people into forsaking the Kaaba, he determined to invade Mecca itself and to destroy the rival place of worship. So he gathered together a great army, which numbered amongst it an elephant, a fearful sight to the Meccans, who had never seen so great an animal. With this force he marched upon Mecca, and was about to enter the city after fruitless attempts by Abd al Muttalib to obtain quarter, when God sent down a scourge of sickness upon his army and he was forced to retreat, returning miserably to Sana with a remnant of his men. But so much had the presence of the elephant alarmed the Meccans that the year (A.D. 570) was called ever after "The Year of the Elephant," and in August thereof Mahomet was born.

Then Amina sent for Abd al Muttalib and told him the marvels she had seen and heard, and his grandfather took the child and presented him in the Kaaba, after the manner of the Jews, and gave him the name Mahomet (the Praised One), according as the angel had commanded Amina.

The countless legends surrounding Mahomet's birth, even to the physical marvel that accompanied it, cannot be set aside as utterly worthless. They serve to show the temper of the nation producing them, deeply imaginative and incoherently poetical, and they indicate the weight of the personality to which they cling. All the devotion of the East informs them; but since the spirit that caused them to be is in its essence one of relentless activity, neither contemplative nor mystic, they lack that subtle sweetness that belongs to the Buddhist and Christian histories, and dwell rather within the region of the marvellous than of the spiritually symbolic. Neither Mahomet's father nor mother are known to us in any detail; they are merely the passive instruments of Mahomet's prophetic mission. His real parents are his grandfather and his uncle Abu Talib; but more than these, the desert that nurtured him, physically and mentally, that bounded his horizon throughout his life and impressed its mighty mysteries upon his unconscious childhood and his eager, imaginative youth.

CHAPTER II

CHILDHOOD

"Paradise lies at the feet of mothers."—MAHOMET.

No more beautiful and tender legends cluster round Mahomet than those which grace his life in the desert under the loving care of his foster-mother Hailima. She was a woman of the tribe of Beni Sa'ad, who for generations had roamed the desert, tent-dwellers, who visited cities but rarely, and kept about them the remoteness and freedom of their adventurous life beneath the sun and stars.

About the time of Mahomet's birth a famine fell upon the Beni Sa'ad, which left nothing of all their stores, and the women of the tribe journeyed,[28] weary and stricken with hunger, into the city of Mecca that they might obtain foster-children whose parents would give them money and blessings if they could but get their little ones taken away from that unhealthy place. Among these was Hailima, who, according to tradition, has left behind her the narrative of that dreadful journey across the desert with her husband and her child, and with only an ass and a she-camel for transport. Famine oppressed them sorely, together with the heat of desert suns, until there was no sustenance for any living creature; then, faint and travel-weary, they reached the city and began their quest.

Mahomet was offered to every woman of the tribe, but they rejected him as he had no father, and there was little hope of much payment from the mothers of these children. Those of rich parents were eagerly spoken for, but no one would care for the little fatherless child. And it happened that Hailima also was unsuccessful in her search, and was like to have returned to her people disconsolate, but when she saw Mahomet she bethought herself and said to her husband:

"By the God of my fathers, I will not go back to my companions without foster-child. I will take this orphan."

And her husband replied: "It cannot harm thee to do this, and if thou takest him it may be that through him God will bless us."

So Hailima took him, and she relates how good fortune attended her from that day. Her camels gave abundant milk during the homeward journey, and in the unfruitful land of the Beni Sa'ad her cattle were always fattest and yielded most milk, until her neighbours besought her to allow them to pasture their cattle with hers. But, adds the chronicler naively, in spite of this their cattle returned to them thin and yielding little, while Hailima's waxed fat and fruitful. These legends are the translation into poetic fact of the peace and love surrounding Mahomet during the five years he spent with Hailima; for in all primitive communities every experience must pass through transmutation into the definite and tangible and be given a local habitation and a name.

When Mahomet was two years old and the time had come to restore him to his mother, Hailima took him back to Mecca; but his mother gave him to her again because he had thriven so well under desert skies, and she feared the stifling air of Mecca for her only son. So Hailima returned with him and brought him up as one of her children until he was five, when the first signs of his nervous, highly-strung nature showed themselves in a kind of epileptic fit. The Arabians, unskilled as they were in any medical science, attributed manifestations of this kind to evil spirits, and it is not surprising that we find Hailima bringing him back to his grandfather in great alarm. So ended his fostering by the desert and by Hailima.

Of these five years spent among the Beni Sa'ad chroniclers have spoken in much detail, but their confused accounts are so interwoven with legend that it is impossible to re-create events, and we can only obtain a general idea of his life as a tiny child among the children of the tribe, sharing their fortunes, playing and quarrelling with them, and at moments, when the spirit seemed to advance beyond its dwelling-place, gazing wide-eyed upon the limitless desert under the blaze of sun or below the velvet dark, with swift, half-conscious questionings uttering the universal why and how [31] of childhood. Legend regards even this early time as one of preparation for his mission, and there are stories of the coming of two men clothed in white and shining garments, who ripped open his body, took out his heart, and having purged it of all unrighteousness, returned it, symbolically cleansing him of sin that he might forward the work of God. It was an imaginative rightness that decreed that Mahomet's most impressionable years should be spent in the great desert, whose twin influences of fierceness and fatalism he felt throughout his life, and which finally became the key-notes of his worship of Allah.

Hailima, convinced that her foster-son was possessed by evil spirits, resolved to return him to Abd al Muttalib, but as she journeyed through Upper Mecca, the child wandered away and was lost for a time. Hailima hurried, much agitated, to his grandfather, who immediately sent his sons to search, and after a short time they returned with the boy, unharmed and unfrightened by his adventure. The legend—it is quite a late accretion—is interesting, as showing an acquaintance with, and a parallelism to, the story of the losing of Jesus among the Passover crowds, and the search for Him by His kindred. Mahomet was at last lodged with his mother, who indignantly explained to Hailima the real meaning of his malady, and spoke of his future glory as manifested to her by the light that enfolded her before his birth. Not long after, Amina decided to visit her

[32] husband's tomb at Medina, and thither Mahomet accompanied her, travelling through the rocky, desolate valleys and hills that separate the two, with just his mother and a slave girl.

Mahomet was too young to remember much about the journey to Medina, except that it was hot and that he was often tired, and since his father was but a name to him, the visit to his tomb faded altogether from his mind. But on the homeward journey a calamity overtook him which he remembered all his life. Amina, weakened by journeying and much sorrow, and perhaps feeling her desire for life forsake her after the fulfillment of her pilgrimage, sickened and died at Abwa, and Mahomet and the slave girl continued their mournful way alone.

Amina is drawn by tradition in very vague outline, and Mahomet's memory of her as given in the Kuran does not throw so much light upon the woman herself as upon her child's devotion and affectionate memory of the mother he lost almost before he knew her. His grief for her was very real; she remained continually in his thoughts, and in after years he paid tribute at her tomb to her tenderness and love for him.

"This is the grave of my mother ... the Lord hath permitted me to visit it.... I called my mother to remembrance, and the tender memory of her overcame me and I wept."

The sensitive, over-nervous child, left thus solitary, away from all his kindred, must have brought back with him to Mecca confused but vivid impressions of the long journey and of the catastrophe which lay at the end of it. The uncertainty of his future, and the joys of gaining at last a foster-father in Abd al Muttalib, finds reflection in the Kuran in one little burst of praise to God: "Did He not find thee an orphan, and furnish thee with a refuge?"

Life for two years as the foster-child of Abd al Muttalib, the venerable, much honoured chief of the house of Hashim, passed very pleasantly for Mahomet. He was the darling of his grandfather's last years of life; for, perhaps having pity on his defencelessness, perhaps divining with that prescience which often marks old age, something of the revelation this child was to be to his countrymen, he protected him from the harshness of his uncles. A rug used to be placed in the shadow of the Kaaba, and there the aged ruler rested during the heat of the day, and his sons sat around him at respectful distance, listening to his words. But the child Mahomet, who loved his grandfather, ran fearlessly up, and would have seated himself by Abd al Muttalib's side. Then the sons sought to punish him for his lack of reverence, but their father prevented them:

"Leave the child in peace. By the God of my fathers, I swear he will one day be a mighty prophet."

So Mahomet remained in close attendance upon the old man, until he died in the eighth year after the Year of the Elephant, and there was mourning for him in the houses of his sons.

When Abd al Muttalib knew his end was near he sent for his daughters, and bade them make lamentation over him. We possess traditional accounts of these funeral songs; they are representative of the wild rhetorical eloquence of the poetry of the day. They lose immensely in translation, and even in reading with the eye instead of hearing, for they were never meant to find immortality in the written words, but in the speech of men.

"When in the night season a voice of loud lament proclaimed the sorrowful tidings I wept, so that the tears ran down my face like pearls. I wept for a noble man, greater than all others, for Sheibar, the generous, endowed with virtues; for my beloved father, the inheritor of all good things, for the man faithful in his own house, who never shrank from combat, who stood fast and needed not a prop, mighty, well-favoured, rich in gifts. If a man could live for ever by reason of his noble nature—but to none is this lot vouchsafed—he would remain untouched of death because of his fair fame and his good deeds."

The songs furnish ample evidence as to the high position which Abd al Muttalib held among the Kureisch. His death was a great loss to his nation, but it was a greater calamity to his little foster-child, for it brought him from ease and riches to comparative poverty and obscurity with his uncle, Abu Talib. None of Abd al Muttalib's sons inherited the nature of their father, and with his death the greatness of the house of Hashim diminished, until it gave place to the Omeyya branch, with Harb at its head. The offices at Mecca were seized by the Omeyya, and to the descendants of Abd al Muttalib there remained but the privilege of caring for the well Zemzem, and of giving its water for the refreshment of pilgrims. Only two of his sons, except Abu Talib, who earns renown chiefly as the guardian of Mahomet, attain anything like prominence. Hamza was converted at the beginning of Mahomet's mission, and continued his helper and warrior until he died in battle for Islam; Abu Lahab (the flame) opposed Mahomet's teaching with a vehemence that earned him one of the fiercest denunciations in the early, passionate Suras of the Kuran:

"Blasted be the hands of Abu Lahab; let himself perish;
His wealth and his gains shall avail him not;
Burned shall he be with the fiery flame,
His wife shall be laden with firewood—
On her neck a rope of palm fibre."

Mahomet, bereft a second time of one he loved and on whom he depended, passed into the care of his uncle, Abu Talib. This was a man of no great force of character, well-disposed and kindly, but of straitened means, and lacking in the qualities that secure success. Later, he seems to have attained a more important position, mainly, one would imagine, through the lion courage and unfaltering faith in the Prophet of his son, the mighty warrior Ali, of whom it is written, "Mahomet is the City of Knowledge, and Ali is the Gate thereof." But although Abu Talib was sufficiently strong to withstand the popular fury of the Kureisch against Mahomet, and to protect him for a time on the grounds of kinship, he never finally decided upon which side he would take his stand. Had he been a far-seeing, imaginative man, able to calculate even a little the force that had entered into Arabian polity, the history of the foundation of Islam would have been continued, with Mecca as its base, and have probably resolved itself into the war of two factions within the city, wherein the new faith, being bound to the more powerful political party, would have had a speedier conquest.

With Abu Talib Mahomet spent the rest of his childhood and youth—quiet years, except for a journey to Syria, and his insignificant part in the war against the Hawazin, a desert tribe that engaged the Kureisch for some time. In Abu Talib's house there was none of the ease that had surrounded him with Abd al Muttalib. But Mahomet was naturally an affectionate child, and was equally attached to his uncle as he had been to his grandfather.

Two years later Abu Talib set out on a mercantile journey, and was minded to leave his small foster-child behind him, but Mahomet came to him as he sat on his camel equipped for his journey, and clinging to him passionately implored his uncle not to go without him. Abu Talib could not resist his pleading, and so Mahomet accompanied him on that magical journey through the desert, so glorious yet awesome to an imaginative child. Bostra was the principal city of exchange for merchandise circulating between Yemen, Northern Arabia, and the cities of Upper Palestine, and Mahomet must thus have travelled on the caravan route through the heart of Syria, past Jerash, Ammon, and the site of the fated Cities of the Plain. In Syria, too, he first encountered the Christian faith, and planted those remembrances that were to be revived and strengthened upon his second journey through that wonderful land—in religion, and in a lesser degree in polity, a law unto itself, forging out its own history apart from the main stream of Christian life and thought.

Legends concerning this journey are rife, and all emphasise the influence Christianity had upon his mind, and also the ready recognition of his coming greatness by all those Christians who saw him. On the homeward journey the monk Bahirah is fabled to have met the party and to have bidden them to a feast. When he saw the child was not among them he was wroth, and commanded his guests to bring "every man of the company." He interrogated Mahomet and Abu Talib concerning the parentage of the boy, and we have here the first traditional record of Mahomet's speech.

"Ask what thou wilt," he said to Bahirah, "and I will make answer."

So Bahirah questioned him as to the signs that had been vouchsafed him, and looking between his shoulders found the seal of the prophetic office, a mole covered with hair. Then Bahirah knew this was he who was foretold, and counselled Abu Talib to take him to his native land, and to beware [39] of the Jews, for he would one day attain high honour. At this time Mahomet was little more than a child, but although few thoughts of God or of human destiny can have crossed his mind, he retained a vivid impression of the storied places through which he passed—Jerash, Ammon, the valley of Hejr, and saw in imagination the mighty stream of the Tigris, the ruinous cities, and Palmyra with its golden pillars fronting the sun. The tribes which the caravan encountered were rich in legend and myth, and their influence, together with the more subtle spell of the desert vastness, wrought in him that fervour of spirit, a leaping, troubled flame, which found mortal expression in the poetry of the early part of the Kuran, where the vision of God's majesty compels the gazer into speech that sweeps from his mind in a stream of fire:

"By the Sun and his noonday brightness,
By the Moon when she followeth him,
By Day when it revealeth his glory,
By the night when it enshroudeth him,
By the Heaven and Him who built it,
By the Earth and Him who spread it forth,
By the Soul and Him who balanced it,
Breathed into its good, yea, and its evil—
Verily man's lot is cast amid destruction
Save those who believe and deal justly,
And enjoin upon each other steadfastness and truth."

CHAPTER III

STRIFE AND MEDITATION

"God hath treasuries beneath the throne, the keys whereof are the tongues of poets."—MAHOMET.

The Arabian calendar has always been in a distinctive manner subject to the religion of the people. Before Mahomet imposed his faith upon Mecca, there were four sacred months following each other, in which no war might be waged. For four months, therefore, the tumultuous Arab spirit was restrained from that most precious to it; pilgrimages to holy places were undertaken, and there was a little leisure for the cultivation of art and learning.

The Greater Pilgrimage to Mecca, comprising the sevenfold circuit of the Kaaba and the kissing of the sacred Black Stone, and culminating in a procession to the holy places of Mina and Arafat, could only be undertaken in Dzul-Higg, corresponding in the time of Mahomet to our March. The month preceding, Dzul-Cada, was occupied in a kind of preparation and rejoicing, which took the form of a fair at Ocatz, three days' journey east of Mecca, when representatives of all the surrounding nations used to assemble to exchange merchandise, to take part in the games, to listen to the contests in poetry and rhetoric, and sometimes to be roused into sinister excitement at the proximity of so many tribes differing from them in nationality, and often in their religion and moral code.

Into this vast concourse came Mahomet, a lad of fifteen, eager to see, hear, and know. He was present at the poetic contests, and caught from the protagonists a reflection of their vivid, fitful eloquence, with its ceaseless undercurrent of monotony.

Romance, in so far as it represents the love of the strange, is a product of the West. There is a rigidity in the Eastern mind that does not allow of much change or seeking after new things. Wild and beautiful as this poetry of Arabia is, its themes and their manner of treatment seldom vary; as the desert is changeless in contour, filled with a brilliant sameness, whirling at times into sombre fury and as suddenly subsiding, so is the literature which it fostered. The monotony is expressed in a reiteration of subject, barbarous to the intellect of the West; endurance is born of that monotony, and strength, and the acquiescence in things as they are, but not the discovery and development of ideas. Arabia does not flash forth a new presentment of beauty, following the vivid apprehension of some lovely form, but broods over it in a kind of slumbering enthusiasm that mounts at last into a glory of metaphor, drowning the subject in intensest light. The rival poets assembled to discover who could turn the deftest phrases in satire of the opposing tribe, or extol most eloquently the bravery and skill of his own people, the beauty and modesty of their women, and from these wild outpourings Mahomet learnt to clothe his thoughts in that splendid garment whose jewels illumine the earlier part of the Kuran.

Perhaps more important than the poetical contests was the religious aspect of the fair at Ocatz. Here were gathered Jew, Christian, and Arabian worshipper of many gods, in a vast hostile confusion. Mahomet was familiar with Jewish cosmogony from his knowledge of their faith within his own land, and he had heard dimly of the Christian principles during his Syrian journey. But here, though both Jews and Christians claimed to be worshippers of a single God, and although the Jews took for their protector Abraham, the mighty founder of Mahomet's own city, yet there was nothing between all the sects but fruitless strife. He saw the Jews looking disdainfully upon the Christian dogs, and the Christians firmly convinced that an irrevocable doom would shortly descend upon every Jew. Both united in condemning to eternal wrath the idol-worshippers of the Kaaba. It was a fiercely outspoken, remorseless enmity that he saw around him, and the impotence born of distrust he saw also.

It is not possible that any hint of his future mission enlightened him as to the part he was to play in eliminating this conflict, but may it not be that there was sown in his mind a seed of thought concerning the uselessness of all this strife of religions, and the limitless power that might accrue to his nation if it could but be persuaded to become united in allegiance to the one true God? For even at that early stage Mahomet, with the examples of Judaism and Christianity before him, must have rejected, even if unthinkingly, the polytheistic idea.

The poetic and warlike contests partook of the fiery earnestness characteristic of the combatants, and it was seldom that the fair at Ocatz passed by without some hostile demonstration. The greatest rivals were the Kureisch and the Hawazin, a tribe dwelling between Mecca and Taif.

The Hawazin were tumultuous and unruly, and the Kureisch ever ready to rouse their hostility by numerous small slights and taunts. We read traditionally of an insult by some Kureisch youths towards a girl of the Hawazin; this incident was closed peaceably, but some years later the Kureisch (always the aggressive party because of their stronghold in Mecca) committed an outrage that could not be passed over. As the fair progressed, news came of the murder of a Hawazin, chief of a caravan, and the seizure of his treasure by an ally of the Kureisch. That tribe, knowing themselves at a disadvantage and fearing vengeance, fled back to Mecca. The Hawazin pursued them remorselessly to the borders of the sacred precincts, beyond which it was sacrilegious to wage war. Some traditions say they followed their foe undaunted by fear of divine wrath, and thus incurred a double disgrace of having fought in the sacred month and within the sacred territory. But their pursuit cannot have lasted long, because we find them challenging the Kureisch to battle at the same time the next year. All Mahomet's uncles took part in the Sacrilegious War that followed, and stirring times continued for Mahomet until a truce was made after four years. He attended his uncles in warfare, and we hear of his collecting the enemy's arrows that fell harmlessly into their lines, in order to reinforce the Kureisch ammunition.

A vivid picture by the hand of tradition is this period in Mahomet's life, for he was between eighteen and nineteen, just at the age when fighting would appeal to his wild, yet determined nature. He must have learned resource and some of the stratagem of war from this attendance upon warriors, if he did not become filled with much physical daring, never one of his characteristics, nor, indeed, of any man of his nervous temperament, and his imagination was certainly kindled by the spectacle of the horrors and triumphs of strife. Several battles were fought with varying success, until at the end of about five years' fighting both sides were weary and a truce was called. It was found that twenty more Hawazin had been killed than Kureisch, and according to the simple yet equitable custom of the time, a like number of hostages was given to the Hawazin that there might not be blood feud between them.

The Kureisch passed as suddenly into peace as they had plunged into strife. After the Sacrilegious War, a period of prosperity began for the city of Mecca. It was wealthy enough to support its population, and trade flourished with the marts of Bostra, Damascus, and Northern Syria. Its political condition had never been very stable, and it seems to have preserved during the Omeyyad ascendancy the same loose but roughly effective organisation that it possessed under the Hashim branch. The intellect that could see the potentialities of such a polity, once it could be knit together by some common bond, had not arisen; but the scene was prepared for his coming, and we have to think of the Mecca of that time as offering untold suggestions for its religious, and later for its political, salvation to a mind anxious to produce, but uncertain as yet of its medium.

Mahomet returned with Abu Talib, and passed with him into obscurity of a poverty not too burdensome, and to a quiet, somewhat reflective household. He lived under the spell of that tranquillity until he was twenty-five, and of this time there is not much notice in the traditions, but its contemplation is revealed to us in the earlier Chapters of the Kuran. At one time Mahomet acted as shepherd upon the Meccan hills—low, rocky ranges covered with a dull scrub, and open to the limitless vaults of sky. Here, whether under sun or stars, he learned that love and awe of Nature that throbs through the early Chapters of the Kuran like a deep organ note of praise, dominated almost always with fear.

"Consider the Heaven—with His Hand has He built it up, and given it its vastness—and the Earth has He stretched out like a carpet, smoothly has He spread it forth! Verily, God is the sole sustainer, possessed of might, the unshaken! Fly then to God."

Indeed, a haunting terror broods over all those souls who know the desert, and this fear translated into action becomes fierce and terrible deeds, and into the world of the spirit, angry dogmatic commands. It is the result of the knowledge that to those who stray from the well-known desert track comes death; equally certain is the destruction of the soul for those who transgress against the law of the Ruler of the earth. The God of the early Kuran is the spiritual representative of the forces surrounding Mahomet, whether of Nature or government. The country around Mecca conveys one central thought to one who meditates—the sense of power, not the might of one kindly and familiar, but the unapproachable sovereignty of one alien and remote, a dweller in far-off places, who nevertheless fills the earth with his dominion. Mahomet passing by, as he did, the gaieties and temptations of youth, had his mind alert for the influences of this Nature, full of awful power, and for the contemplation of life and the Universe around him.

In common with many enthusiasts and men of action, certain sides of his nature, especially the sexual and the practical, awoke late, and were preceded by a reflective period wherein the poet held full sway. He never desired the companionship of those of his own age and their rather debased pleasures. There are legends of his being miraculously preserved from the corruption of the youthful vices of Mecca, but the more probable reason for his shunning them is that they made no appeal to his desires. Some minds and tastes unfold by imperceptible degrees—flowers that attain fruition by the shedding of their earlier petals. Mahomet was of this nature. At this time the poet was paramount in his mental activities He loved silence and solitude, so that he might use those imaginative and contemplative gifts of which he felt himself to possess so large a share.

It is not possible at this distance of time to attempt to estimate the importance of this period in Mahomet's mental development. There are not sufficient data to enable history to fill in any detailed sketch, but the outlines may be safely indicated by the help of his later life and the testimony of that commentary upon his feelings and actions, the Kuran. His nature now seems to be in a pause of expectation, whose vain urgency lasted until he became convinced of his prophetic mission. He must have been at this time the seeker, whose youth, if not his very eagerness, prevented his attaining what he sought. He was earnest and sincere, grave beyond his years, and so gained from his fellows the respect always meted out, in an essentially religion-loving community, to any who give promise of future "inspiration," before its actuality has rendered him too uncomfortable a citizen. He received from his comrades the title of Al-Amin (the Faithful), and continued his life apart from his kind, performing his duties well, but still remaining aloof from others as one not of their world. From his sojourn in the mountains came the inspiration that created the poetry of the Kuran and the reflective interest in what he knew of his world and its religion; both embryos, but especially the latter, germinated in his mind until they emerged into full consciousness and became his fire of religious conviction, and his zeal for the foundation and glory of Islam.

CHAPTER IV

ADVENTURE AND SECURITY

"Women are the twin-halves of men."—MAHOMET.

Abu Talib's straitened circumstances never prevented him from treating his foster-child with all the affection of which his kindly but somewhat weak character was capable. But the cares of a growing family soon became too much for his means, and when Mahomet was about twenty-five his uncle suggested that he should embark upon a mercantile journey for some rich trader in Mecca. We can imagine Mahomet, immersed in his solitudes, responding reluctantly to a call that could not be evaded. He was not by nature a trader, and the proposal was repugnant to him, except for his desire to help his uncle, and more than this, his curiosity to revisit at a more assimilative age the lands that he remembered dimly from childhood.

Khadijah, a beautiful widow, daughter of an honoured house and the cousin of Mahomet, rich and much sought after by the Kureisch, desired someone to accompany her trading venture to Bostra, and hearing of the wisdom and faithfulness of Mahomet, sent for him, asking if he would travel for her into Syria and pursue her bargains in that northern city. She was willing to reward him far more generously than most merchants. Mahomet, anxious to requite his uncle in some way, and with his young imagination kindled at the prospect of new scenes and ideas, prepared eagerly for the journey. With one other man-servant, Meisara, he set out with the merchandise to Bostra, traversing as a young man the same desert path he had journeyed along in boyhood.

He was of an age to appreciate all that this experience could teach, in the regions both of Nature and religion. The lonely desert only increased his pervading sense of the mystery lying beyond his immediate knowledge, and its vastness confirmed his vague belief in some kind of a power who alone controlled so mighty a creation as the abounding spaces around him, and the "star-bespangled" heaven above. On this journey, too, he first saw with conscious eyes the desert storms in all the splendour and terror of their fury, and caught the significance of those sudden squalls that urge the waters of the upper Syrian lakes into a tumult of destruction. Frequent allusions to sea and lake storms are to be found in the earlier part of the Kuran: "When the seas shall be commingled, when the seas shall boil, then shall man tremble before his creator." "By the swollen sea, verily a chastisement from thy Lord is imminent." In every natural manifestation that struck Mahomet's imagination in these early days, God appeared to him as the sovereign of power, as terrible and as remote as He was in the lightnings on Sinai. What wonder, then, that when the call came to him to take up his mission it became a command to "arise and warn"?

The chroniclers would have us believe that his contact with Christianity was more important than his communion with Nature. Most of the legends surrounding his relations with Christian Syria may be safely accepted as later additions, but it is certain that he paid some attention to the religion of those people through whose country he passed. A Syrian monk is said to have seen Mahomet sitting beneath a tree, and to have hailed him as a prophet; there is even a traditional account of an interview with Nestorius, but this must be set aside at once as pure fiction.

The kernel of these legends seems to be the desire to show that Mahomet had studied Christianity, and was not imposing a new religion without having considered the potentialities of those already existing. However that may be, Christianity certainly interested Mahomet, and must have influenced him towards the monotheistic idea. The Arabians themselves were not entirely ignorant of it; they witnessed the worship of one God by the Jews and Christians on the borders of their territory, and although it is a very debatable point how far the idea of one God had progressed in Arabia when Mahomet began his mission, it may fairly be accepted that dissatisfaction with the old tribal gods was not wanting. Mahomet saw the countries through which he passed in a state of religious flux, and heard around him diverse creeds, detecting doubtless an undercurrent of unrest and a desire for some religion of more compelling power.

With the single slave he reached Bostra in safety with the merchandise, and having concluded his barter very successfully, and retaining in his mind many impressions of that crowded city, returned to Mecca by the same desert route. Meisara, the slave, relates (in what is doubtless a later addition) of the fierce noonday heat that beset the travellers, and how, when Mahomet was almost exhausted, two angels sat on his camel and protected him with their wings. When they reached Mecca, Khadijah sold the merchandise and found her wealth doubled, so careful had Mahomet been to ensure the prosperity of his client, and before long love grew up in her heart for this tall, grave youth, who was faithful in small things as well as in great.

Khadijah had been much sought after by the men of Mecca, both for her riches and for her beauty, but she had preferred to remain independent, and continued her orderly life among her maidens, attending to her household, and finding enough occupation in the supervision of her many mercantile ventures. She was about forty, fair of countenance, and gifted with a rich nature, whose leading qualities were affection and sympathy. She seems to have been pre-eminently one of those receptive women who are good to consult for the clarification of ideas. Her intelligence was quick to grasp another's thought, if she did not originate thought within herself. She was a woman fitted to be the helper and guide of such a man as Mahomet, eager, impulsive, prone to swiftly alternating extremes of depression and elation. A subtle mental attraction drew them together, and Khadijah divined intuitively the power lying within the mind of this youth and also his need of her, both mentally and materially, to enable him to realise his whole self. Therefore as she was the first to awaken to her desire for him, the first advances come from her.

She sent her sister to Mahomet to induce him to change his mind upon the subject of marriage, and when he found that the rich and gracious Khadijah offered him her hand, he could not believe his good fortune, and assured the sister that he was eager to make her his wife. The alliance, in spite of its personal suitability, was far from being advantageous to Khadijah from a worldly point of view, and the traditions of how her father's consent was obtained have all the savour of contemporary evidence.

The father was bidden to a feast, and there plied right royally with wine. When his reason returned he asked the meaning of the great spread of viands, the canopy, and the chapleted heads of the guests. Thereupon he was told it was the marriage-feast of Mahomet and Khadijah, and his wrath and amazement were great, for had he not by his presence given sanction to the nuptials? The incident throws some light upon the marriage laws current at the time. Khadijah, though forty and a widow, was still under the guardianship of her father, having passed to him after the death of her husband, and his consent was needed before she married again.

The marriage contracted by mutual desire was followed by a time of leisure and happiness, which Mahomet remembered all his life. Never did any man feel his marriage gift (in Mahomet's case twenty young camels) more fitly given than the youth whom Khudijah rescued from poverty, and to whom she gave the boon of her companionship and counsel. The marriage was fruitful; two sons were born, the eldest Kasim, wherefore Mahomet received the title of Abu-el-Kasim, the father of Kasim, but both these died in infancy. There were also four daughters born to Mahomet—Zeineb, Rockeya, Umm Kolthum, and Fatima. These were important later on for the marriages they contracted with Mahomet's supporters, and indeed his whole position was considerably solidified by the alliances between his daughters and his chief adherents.

Ten years passed thus in prosperity and study. Mahomet was no longer obscure but the chief of a wealthy house, revered for his piety, and looked upon already as one of those "to whom God whispers in the ear." His character now exhibited more than ever the marks of the poet and seer; the time was at hand when all the subdued enthusiasm of his mind was to break forth in the opening Suras of the Kuran. The inspiration had not yet descended upon him, but it was imminent, and the shadow of its stern requirements was about him as he attended to his work of supervising Khadijah's wealth or took part in the religious life of Mecca.

In A.D. 605, when Mahomet was thirty-five years old, the chief men of Mecca decided to rebuild the Kaaba. The story of its rebuilding is perhaps the most interesting of the many strange, naive tales of this adventurous city. Valley floods had shattered the house of the gods. It was roofless, and so insecure that its treasury had already been rifled by blasphemous men. It stood only as high as the stature of a man, and was made simply of stones laid one above the other. Rebuilding was absolutely necessary, but materials were needed before the work could begin, and this delayed the Kureisch until chance provided them with means of accomplishing their design. A Grecian ship had been driven in a Red Sea storm upon the coast near Mecca and was rapidly being broken up. When the Kureisch heard of it, they set out in a body to the seashore and took away the wood of the ship to build a roof for the Kaaba. It is a significant fact that tradition puts a Greek carpenter in Mecca who was able to advise them as to the construction. The Meccans themselves were not sufficiently skilled in the art of building.

But now a great difficulty awaited them. Who was to undertake the responsibility of demolishing so holy a place, even if it were only that it might be rebuilt more fittingly? Many legends cluster round the demolition. It would seem that the gods only understood gradually that a complete destruction of the Kaaba was not intended. Their opposition was at first implacable. The loosened stones flew back into their places, and finally none could be induced to make the attempt to pull down the Kaaba. There was a pause in the work, during which no one dared venture near the temple, then Al-Welid, being a bold and god-fearing spirit, took an axe, and crying:

"I will make a beginning, let no evil ensue, O Lord!" he began to dislodge the stones.

Then the rest of the Kureisch rather cravenly waited until the next day, but seeing that no calamity had befallen Al-Welid, they were ready to continue the work. The rebuilding prospered until they came to a point where the Black Stone must be embedded in the eastern wall.

At this juncture a vehement dispute arose among the Kureisch as to who was to have the honour of depositing the Black Stone in its place. They wrangled for days, and finally decided to appeal to Mahomet, who had a reputation for wisdom and resource. Mahomet, after carefully considering the question, ordered a large cloth to be brought, and commanded the representatives of the four chief Meccan houses to hold each a corner. Then he deposited the Black Stone in the centre of it, and in this manner, with the help of every party in the quarrel, the sacred object was raised to the proper height. When this was done Mahomet conducted the Black Stone to its niche in the wall with his own hand.

The building of the Kaaba was ultimately completed, and a great festival was held in honour. Many hymns of praise were sung at the accomplishment of so difficult and important a work. The Kaaba has remained substantially the same as it was when it was first rebuilt. It is a small place of no architectural pretensions, merely a square with no windows, and a tiny door raised from the ground, by which the Faithful, duly prepared, are allowed to enter upon rare occasions. The sacred Black Stone lies embedded about three feet from the ground in the eastern wall, at first a dark greenish stone of volcanic or aerolitic origin, now worn black and polished by thousands of kisses. There is little in the Kaaba to account for the reverence bestowed upon it, and its insignificance bears witness to the Eastern capacity for worshipping the idea for which its symbols stand. This was the sacred temple of Abraham and Ishmael, therefore its exterior mattered little.

Mahomet's share in the construction of the Kaaba brought him further honour among the Kureisch. From this time until the beginning of his mission he lived a quiet, easeful domestic life, interrupted only by mental storms and depressions. He found leisure to meditate and observe, and of this necessarily uneventful time there is little or no mention in the histories. He certainly gained an opportunity of examining somewhat closely the tenets of Christianity by the entrance into his household of Zeid, a Christian slave, cultured and well-informed as to the doctrines of his religion, and his presence doubtless influenced Mahomet in the spiritual battles he encountered at a time when as yet he was certain neither of God nor himself. Besides Zeid another important personage entered Mahomet's household, Ali, son of Abu Talib, and future convert and pride of Islam, "the lion of the Faith." The adoption of Ali was Mahomet's small recompense to Abu Talib for his care of him, and the advantages there from to Islam were inestimable. Ali was no statesman, but he was an indomitable fighter, with whose aid Mahomet founded his religion of the sword.

In such quiet manner Mahomet passed the years immediately preceding the discovery of his mission, and as religious doubts and fears alternated in him with fervour and hopefulness, so signs were not wanting of a spirit of inquiry found abroad in Arabia, discontented with the old religions, seeking for a clearer enthusiasm and withheld from its goal. Legends gather round the figures of four inquirers who are reputed to have come to Mahomet for enlightenment, and the story is but the primitive device of rendering concrete and material all those vague stirrings of the communal spirit towards a more convincing conception of the world— legends that embody ideas in personalities, mainly because their language has no words for the expression of the abstract, and also that, clothed in living garments, they may capture the hearts of men. The time for the coming of a prophet and a teacher could not be long delayed, and a foreboding of his imperious destiny, dark with war and aflame with God's judgment, had already begun to steal across Mahomet's hesitant soul.

CHAPTER V

INSPIRATION

"Recite thou in the name of thy Lord who created,
Yan, who hath made man from Clots of Blood,
Recite thou, for thy Lord, he is most bounteous."
The Kuran.

The mental growth by which Mahomet attained the capacity of Prophet and ruler will always have spread about it a misty veil, wherein strange shapes and awful visions are dimly discerned. Did his soul face the blankness that baffles and entices the human spirit with any convictions, the gradual products of thought and experience, or was it with an unmeaning chaos within him that he stumbled into faith and evolved his own creed? His knowledge of Christianity and Judaism undoubtedly helped to foster in him his central idea of the indivisibility of God. But how was this faith wrought out into his conception of himself as the Prophet of his people?

It is impossible for any decision to be made as to the mainspring of his beliefs, except in the light of his character and development of mind. He was passionate and yet practical, holding within himself the elements of seer and statesman, prophet and law-giver, as yet doubtful of the voice which inspired him, but spurred on in his quest for the truth by an intensity of spirit that carried him forward resistlessly as soon as conviction came to him. The man who imposed his dauntless determination upon a whole people, who founded a system of religious and social laws, who moved armies to fight primarily for an idea, could not lightly gain is right to exhort and control. His nature is almost cataclysmic, and once filled with the fire of the Lord, he bursts forth among his fellow-men "with the right hand striking," to use his own vivid metaphor, but before this evidence of power has come an agonising period of doubt.

Traces of his mental turmoil are seen abundantly in his physical nature. We read of his exhaustion after the inspiration comes, and of "the terrific Suras" that took their toll of his vitality afterwards. The mission imposed upon him was no light burden, and demanded of him strength both of body and mind. The successive stages by which he became convinced of his divine call are only detailed in the histories with the concurrence of the supernatural; he sees material visions and dreams fervent dreams. With the ecstacy of Heaven about him, according to legend, he holds converse with the angel Gabriel, arch-messenger of God, and the divine injunctions must be translated into mental enthusiasms before the true evolution of Mahomet's mind can be dimly conceived.

When he was forty he sought solitude more constantly than formerly. There were deeps in his own nature of which he was only now becoming aware. A restlessness of mind beset him, and continually he retired to a cave at the base of Mount Hira, where he could meditate undisturbed. This mountain, hallowed for ever by the followers of Islam, is now called somewhat ironically, considering its natural barrenness, Jebel Nur, the mountain of Light. Mahomet was of a nervous temperament, the nature that suffers more intensely through its imaginative foresight than in actual experience. He was of those who see keenly and feel towards their beliefs. His faith in God produced none of that self-abnegating rapture to be found in the devotions of many early Christians; it was a personal passion, sweeping up his whole nature within its folds, and rousing the enfolded not to meditation but to instant action.

Through all the legendary accounts there beats that excitement that tells of a mind wrought to the highest pitch, afire with visions, alive with desire. Then, when his fervour attained its zenith, Gabriel came to him in sleep with a silken cloth in his hand covered with writing and said to Mahomet:

"Read!"

"I cannot read."

Then the angel wrapped the cloth about him and once more commanded, "Read!"

Again came the answer, "I cannot read," and again the angel covered him, still repeating, "Read!"

Then his mouth was opened and he read the first sura of the Kuran: "Recite thou in the name of thy Lord who created thee," and when he awoke it seemed to him that these words were graven upon his heart.

Mahomet went immediately up into the mountain, and there Gabriel appeared to him waking and said:

"Thou art God's Prophet, and I am Gabriel."

The archangel vanished, but Mahomet remained rooted to the spot, until Khadijah's messengers found him and brought him to her. The simple story of Mahomet's call to the prophetic office from the lips of the old chroniclers is peculiarly fragrant, but it leaves us in considerable doubt as to the real means by which he attained his faith and was emboldened to preach to his people. It is certain that he had no idea at the time when he received his inspiration, of the ultimate political role in store for him. He was now simply the man who warned the people of their sins, and who insisted upon the sovereignty of one God. Very little argument is ever used by Mahomet to spread his faith. He spoke a plain message, and those who disregarded it were infallibly doomed. He saw himself in the forefront as the man who knew God, and strove to win his countrymen to right ways of life; he did not see himself at the head of earthly armies, controlling the nucleus of a mighty and united Arabia, and until his flight from Mecca to Medina he regarded himself merely as a religious teacher, the political side of his mission growing out of the exigencies of circumstance, almost without his own volition.

His exaltation upon the mountain of light soon faded into uncertainty and fearfulness before the influence of the world's harsh wisdom. Mahomet entered upon a period of hesitation and dreariness, doubtful of himself, of his vision, and of the divine favour. His soul voyaged on dark and troubled seas and gazed into abysmal spaces. At one time he would receive the light of the seven Heavens within his mind, and feel upon him the fervour of the Hebrew prophets of old, and again he would call in vain upon God, and, and seeking, would be flung back upon a darkness of doubt more terrible than the lightnings of divine wrath.

In all those exaltations and glooms Khadijah had part; she comforted his distress and shared his elation until the sorrowful period of the Fattrah, the pause in the revelation, was past. The period is variously estimated by the chroniclers, and there are many nebulous and spurious legends attaching to it, but whatever its length it seems certain that Mahomet gained within it a fuller knowledge of Jewish and Christian tenets, probably through Zeid, the Christian slave in his household, and most accounts agree that the Fattrah was ended by the revelation of the sura entitled "The Enwrapped," the mandate of the angel Gabriel:

"O thou enwrapped in thy mantle,
Arise and warn!"

The explanation of the term "enwrapped in thy mantle" shows the prevailing belief in good and evil spirits characteristic of Mahomet's time. Wandering on the mountain, he saw in a vision the angel Gabriel seated on a throne between heaven and earth, and afraid before so much glory, ran to Khadijah, beseeching her to cover him with his mantle that the evil spirits whom he felt so near him might be avoided. Thereupon Gabriel came down to earth and revealed the Sura of Admonition. This supernatural command would appear to be the translation into the imaginative world of the peace of mind that descended upon Mahomet, and the conviction as to the reality of his inspiration following on a time of despair.

The command fell to one who was peculiarly fitted by nature and circumstance to obey it effectively. To Mahomet, who knew somewhat the chaos of religions around him—Pagan, Jewish, and Christian struggling together in unholy strife—the conception of God's unity, once it attained the strength of a conviction, necessarily resolved itself into an admonitory mission. "There is no God but God," therefore all who believe otherwise have incurred His wrath; hasten then to warn men of their sins. So his conviction passed out of the region of thought into action and received upon it the stamp of time and place, becoming thereby inevitably more circumscribed and intense.

From now onwards the course of Mahomet's life is rendered indisputably plainer by our possession of that famous and much-maligned document, the Kuran, virtually a record of his inspired sayings as remembered and written down by his immediate successors. Apart from its intrinsic value as the universally recognised vehicle of the Islamic creed, it is of immense importance as a commentary upon Mahomet's career. When allowance has been made for its numberless contradictions and repetitions, it still remains the best means of tracing Mahomet's mental development, as well as the course of his religious and political dominance. Although the original document was compiled regardless of chronology, expert scholarship has succeeded in determining the order of most of it contents, and if we cannot say the precise sequence of every sura, at least we can classify each as belonging to one of the two great periods, the Meccan and Medinan, and may even distinguish with comparative accuracy three divisions within the former.

After Mahomet's mandate to preach and warn his fellow-men of their peril, the suras continue intermittently throughout his life. Those of the first period, when his mission was hardly accepted outside his family, bear upon them the stamp of a fiery nature, obsessed with its one idea; but behind the wild words lies a store of energy as yet undiscovered, which will find no fulfilment but in action. That zeal for an idea which caused the Kuran to be, expressed itself at first in words alone, but later was translated into political action, and it is the emptying of this vitality from his words into his works that is responsible for the contrasting prose of the later suras.

But no lack of poetic fire is discernible in the suras immediately following his call to the prophetic office, and from them much may be gathered as to the depth and intensity of his faith. They are almost strident with feeling; his sentences fall like blows upon an anvil, crude in their emphasis, and so swiftly uttered forth from the flame of his zeal, that they glow with reflected glory:

"Say, he is God alone,
God the Eternal,
He begetteth not and is not begotten,
There is none like to Him."

"Verily, we have caused It (the Kuran) to descend on the night of power,
And who shall teach thee what the Night of Power is?
The Night of Power excelleth a thousand months,
Therein descend the angels and the spirit by permission of the Lord."

"By the snorting Chargers,
By those that breathe forth sparks of fire
And those that rush to the attack at morn!

And stir therein the dust aloft,
Cleaving their midmost passage through a host!
Truly man is to his Lord ungrateful,
And of this is himself a witness;
And truly he is covetous in love of this world's good.
Ah, knoweth he not, that when what lies in the grave shall be bared
And that brought forth that is in men's breasts,
Verily in that day shall the Lord be made wise concerning them?"

After the first fire of prophetic zeal had illuminated him, Mahomet devoted himself to the conversion of his own household and family. Khadijah was the first convert, as might have been expected from the close interdependence of their minds. She had become initiated into his prophetship almost equally with her husband, and it was her courage and firm trust in his inspiration that had sustained him during the terrible period of negation. Zeid, the Christian slave who had helped to mould Mahomet's thought by his knowledge of Christian doctrine, was his next convert, but both of these were eclipsed by the devotion to Mahomet's gospel of Ali, the future warrior, son of Abu Talib, and one destined to play a foremost part in the foundation of Islam.

Mahomet's gospel then penetrated beyond the confines of his household with the conversion of his friend Abu Bekr, a successful merchant living in the same quarter of the town as the Prophet. Abu Bekr, whose honesty gained him the title of Al-Siddick (the true), and Ali were by far the most important of Mahomet's "companions." They helped to rule Islam during Mahomet's lifetime, and after his death took successive charge of its fortunes. Ali was too young at this time to manifest his qualities as warrior and ruler, but Abu Bekr was of middle age, and his nature remained substantially the same as at the inception of Islam. He was of short stature, with deep-seated eyes and a thoughtful, somewhat undecided mouth, by nature he was shrewd and intelligent, but possessed little of that original genius necessary to statesmanship in troublous times. His mild, sympathetic character endured him to his fellow-men, and his calm reasonableness earned the gratitude of all who confided in him. He was never ruled by impulse, and of the fire burning almost indestructibly within Mahomet he knew nothing.

It is strange to consider what agency brought these two dissimilar souls into such close relationship. For the rest of his life Mahomet found a never-failing friend in Abu Bekr, and the attachment between the two, apart from their common fount of zeal for Islam, must have been such as is inspired by those of contrasting nature for each other. Mahomet saw a kindly, almost commonplace man, in whose sweet sanity his troubled soul could find a little peace. He was burdened at times with over-resolve that ate into his mind like acid. In Abu Bekr he could find the soothing influence he so often needed, and after the death of Khadijah this friend might be said in a measure to take her place. Abu Bekr, on the other hand, revered his leader as a man of finer, subtler stuff than himself, more alive to the virtue of speed, filled with a greater daring and a profounder impulse than he was. Mahomet, in common with most men meriting the title of great, had a capacity for lifelong friendships as well as the power of inspiring belief and devotion in others.

Through Abu Bekr five converts were gained for the new religion, of whom Othman is the most important. His part in the establishment of the Islamic dominion was no slight one, but at the present he remains simply one of the early enthusiastic converts to Mahomet's evangel, while he enwound himself into the fortunes of his teacher by marrying Rockeya, one of Mahomet's daughters.

The conversion to Islam proceeded slowly but surely among the Kureisch; several slaves were won over, but at the end of four years only forty converts had been made, among whom, however, was Bilal, a slave, who later became the first Muaddzin, or summoner to prayer. During these four years the suras of the first Meccan period were revealed, and enough may be gathered from them to judge both the limits of Mahomet's preaching and the attitude towards it on the part of the Kureisch.

Mahomet was content at this time to emphasise in eloquent, almost incoherent words his central theme—the unity of God. He calls upon the people to believe, and warns them of their fate if they refuse. The suras indicate the attitude of indifference borne by the Kureisch towards Mahomet's mission at its inception. Wherever there are denunciatory suras, they are either for the chastisement of unbelievers or, as in Sura cxi, in revenge for the refusal of his relations to believe in his inspiration. Prophecies of bliss in store for the Faithful are frequent, and of the corresponding woe for Unbelievers. The whole is permeated with the spirit of the poet and visionary, a poetry tumultuous but strong, a vision lurid but inspiring.

The little band of converts under guidance of this fierce rhetoric became united and strengthened in its faith, prepared to defend it, and to spread it as far as possible throughout their kindred.

About three years after Mahomet's receipt of his mission, in A.D. 618, an important change came over the attitude of the Kureisch towards Islam. Hitherto they had jeered or remained indifferent. Mahomet's uncles, Abu Talib and Abu Lahab, represented the two poles of Kureischite feeling. Abu Talib remained untouched by the new faith, but his kindly nature did not allow him to adopt any severe measures for its repression, and, moreover, Mahomet was of his kindred, and he was willing to afford him protection in case of need. Abu Lahab jeered openly, and manifested his scorn by definite speeches. But as the bands of converts grew, the Kureisch found it undesirable to maintain their indifferent attitude. They began to persecute, first refusing to allow the Believers to meet, and then seeking them out individually to endeavour to torture them into recanting.

From this time dates the creation of one of the foremost principles in the creed of the Prophet. If a Believer is in danger of torture, he may dissemble his faith to save himself from infamy and death. Though in striking contrast to the Christian tenets, this exhortation was neither cowardly nor imprudent. In his eyes reckless courting of death would not avail the propagation of Islam, and though a man might die to some good service on the battlefield, smiting his enemies, no wise end could be served when his death would merely gratify the lust of his murderers.

The persecution continued in spite of Mahomet's attempts to withstand it, until he was forced to go to Abu Talib for protection. This was accorded willingly, on account of kindred ties, but there can have been little cordiality between uncle and nephew on the subject, for Mahomet was more than ever determined upon the maintenance and growth of his principles. Still the conversions to Islam continued, and the persecution of its adherents, until there came to the Kureisch a sharp intimation that this new sect arisen in their midst was not an ephemeral affair of a few weeks, but a prolonged endeavour to pursue the ideal of a single God. In 615 the first company of Muslim converts broke from the confined religious area of Mecca and journeyed into Abyssinia, where they could practice their faith in peace. This move convinced the Kureisch of the sincerity of their opponents, for they were almost strong enough to merit the name, and compelled them to believe a little in the force lying behind this strange manifestation of religious zeal in their midst.

Mahomet does not at this time seem to have been definitely ranged against the Kureisch. He was still on negotiable terms with them, and they were a little distrustful of his capacity and ignorant of his power. The stages by which he developed from a discredited citizen, obsessed by one idea, into a political opponent worthy of their best steel and bravest men was necessarily gradual, and indeed the Prophet himself had no knowledge of the role marked out for him by his own personality and the destinies of Arabia. The cause of Islam stood as yet in parlous condition, half-formulated, unwieldy, awaiting the moulding hand of persecution to develop it into a political and social system.

CHAPTER VI

SEVERANCE

"Do you see Al-Lat and Al-Ozza and Manat the third idol beside? These are the exalted females, and truly their intercession is to be expected."—*The Kuran* (last two lines excised later by Mahomet).

The little band of converts, driven by the Kureisch to seek peace and freedom in Abyssinia, remained for two years in their country of refuge, but in 615 returned to Mecca for reasons which have never been fully explained, though it is easy, in the light of future events, to discover the motive behind such a move.

Mahomet was not yet convinced of the impossibility of compromise, neither was the powerful party among the Kureisch utterly indifferent to Mahomet's ancestry as a member of the house of Hashim, and his position as the husband of Khadijah. He had been respected among men for his uprightness before he affronted their prejudices by scorning their gods. His power was daily becoming a source of strife and faction within the city, and the Kureisch were not averse from attempting to come to terms. Mahomet for his part, as far as the scanty evidence of history unfolds his state of mind, seems to have been almost desperately anxious to effect an understanding with the Kureisch. His cause still journeyed by perilous ways, and at the time hopes of his future achievement were apparently dependent upon the goodwill of the dominant Meccan party.

The story runs that the chief men of Mecca were discussing within the Kaaba the affairs of the city. Mahomet came to them and recited Sura liii—The Star—a fulgent psalm in praise of God and heavenly joys. When he came to the verses:

"Do you see Al-Lat and Al-Ozza and Manat the third beside," he inserted:

"Verily these are the exalted females, and truly their intercession may be expected."

They Kureisch were rejoiced at this homage to their deities, and speedily welcomed Mahomet's change of front; but he, disquieted, returned moodily to his house, where Gabriel appeared to him in stern rebuke:

"Thou hast repeated before the people words I never gave to thee."

And Mahomet, whether conscience-stricken by his lapse from the Muslim faith, or convinced that compromise with the Kureisch was impossible and also undesirable in face of his growing power, quickly repudiated the whole affair, which had been unquestionably born of impulse, or possibly an adventurous mood that prompted him "to see what would happen" if he ministered to the prejudices of the Kureisch. It must be acknowledged, however, that repentance for his homage to heathen idols was the mainspring of his recantation, for the period immediately following was one of hardship and persecution for him, and his transitory lapse injured his cause appreciably with the brethren of his faith. The attempt was honourably made, and only failed by Mahomet's swift realisation that his acknowledgment of Lat and Ozza as spirits sanctioned the worship of their images by his fellow-citizens, and this his stern monotheism could not for a moment entertain.

The Muslim, with numbers that increased very slowly, were harried afresh by the Kureisch as soon as Mahomet had withdrawn his concessions, and most of them were forced at length to return to Abyssinia. His pathetic little band, wandering from city to city, doubtful of ever attaining security and uncertain of its ultimate destiny, was the prototype in its vagrancy of that larger and confident band which cast aside its traditions and the city of its birth, headed by a spirit heroic in disaster and supreme in faith, to find its goal in the foundation of a new order for Arabia. Chief among them were Othman and Rockeya, and these were the only ones who returned to Mecca, for the rest remained in Abyssinia until after the migration to Medina, in fact until after Mahomet had carried out the expedition to Kheibar.

Left without any supporters within the city, Mahomet was exposed to all the vituperations and insults which his recent refusal of compromise had brought him. The Kureisch now directed all their energies towards persuading Abu Talib to repudiate his nephew. If once this could be effected, the Kureisch would have a free hand to pursue their desire to exterminate the Muslim and to overthrow the Prophet's power. He was immune from bodily attack, chiefly because of Abu Talib's position in the city as nominal head of the house of Hashim. No Kureisch could run the risk of alienating so great a number of fellow-citizens, and a personal attack upon Abu Talib's nephew could but have that result.

Dark and stormy as the Muslim destiny appeared during this period of transition from religious to political conceptions, nevertheless it was now enriched by the conversion of two of the most influential characters upon its later fortunes—Hamza and Omar. Many stories have been woven round their discovery of the truth of Islam, and by reading between the lines later commentators may discover the forces at work to induce them to take this dubious step. It is beyond question that Mahomet's personality was the moving factor in the conversion of each, for each relates an incident which serves peculiarly to illustrate the Prophet's magnetism.

Hamza, "the lion of God," and a son of Abd-al-Muttalib in his old age, was accosted by a slave girl as he passed on his way through the city She told him breathlessly that she had seen "the Lord Mahomet" insulted and reviled by Abu Jahl, and being unprotected and alone, he could only suffer in silence. Hamza listened to her story with indignation, and determined to revenge the insult to his uncle and foster-brother, for by the ties of kinship they were one. In the Kaaba he publicly declared his allegiance to Islam, and revenged upon Abu Jahl the injuries he had inflicted upon his kinsman. Hamza never repented of his championship of Mahomet. The adventurous fortunes of Islam satisfied his warrior-spirit, and under Mahomet's guidance he helped to control and direct its military zeal, until it had perforce established its religion through the sword. Mahomet's personal magnetism had drawn him irresistibly to the religion he upheld so steadfastly, and in the face of revilement and danger.

Omar was Mahomet's bitterest enemy, and had proved his ability by his persistent opposition to Islam. He was feared by all the company of religionists that had taken up their precarious quarters near Mahomet. He was visiting the house of his sister Fatima when he heard murmurs of someone reciting. He inquired what it was, and learned with anger that it was the Sacred Book of the abhorred Muslim sect. His sister and Zeid, her husband, tremblingly confessed their adherence to Islam, and awaited in terror the probable result. Omar was about to fall upon Zeid, but his wife interposed and received the blow herself. At the sight of his sister's blood Omar paused and then asked for the volume, so that he might judge the message for himself, for he was a writer of no mean standing. Fatima insisted that he should first perform ablutions, so that his touch might not defile the Sacred Book.

Then Omar took it and read it, and the strength and beauty of it smote him. He felt upon him the insistence of a divine command, and straightway asked to be led before Mahomet that he might unburden his conviction to him. He girt on his sword and came to the Prophet's house. As he rapped upon the door a Companion of Mahomet's looked through the lattice, and at the sight of Omar with buckled sword fled in despair to his master. But Mahomet replied:

"Let him enter; if he bring good tidings we will reward him; if he bring bad news, we will smite him, yea, with his own sword."

So the door was opened and Mahomet advanced, asking what was his mission. Omar answered:

"O Prophet of God, I am come to confess that I believe in Allah and in his Prophet."

"Allah Akbar!" (God is great) replied Mahomet gravely, and all the household knew that Omar had become one of themselves.

The conversion of Omar was infinitely important to Islam, and the adherence of this impetuous and dauntless mind was directly due to the strength and steadfastness of Mahomet's faith in himself and his message. Omar was an influential personage among the Kureisch, quick-tempered, but keen as steel, and rejoicing in strife; he stands out among the many warrior-souls to whom Islam gave the opportunity of tasting in its fullness "the splendour of spears." Mahomet had indeed gathered around him a group of men who were remarkable for their character and influence upon Islam. Ali, the warrior par excellence, Abu Bekr, statesman and counsellor, Othman the soldier, Hamza and Omar, are not merely blind followers, but forceful personalities, contributing each in his own manner towards those assets of endurance, leadership, and unshaken faith which ensured the continuance of the Medinan colony and its ultimate victory over the Kureisch.

Omar's conversion did not have the effect of softening the Kureischite fury. On the contrary, the event seems to have stimulated them to further persecution, as if they had some foreshadowings of their waning power, and had determined with a desperate energy to quell for ever, if it might be, this discord in their midst. Their next step was to try an introduce the political element into this conflict of faiths by putting a ban upon the house of Hashim and confining it to Abu Talib's quarter of Sheb. This act, instigated mainly by Abu Jahl, who now becomes prominent as the most terrible of Mahomet's persecutors, had a very notable effect upon his position as well as upon the qualities of the cause for which his party was contending.

For the first time the political aspect of Islam obtrudes itself. Mahomet's followers are now not only the opponents of the Kureischite faith and the enemies of their idols, but they are also their political foes, and have drawn the whole house of Hashim into faction against the ruling power—the Omeyyad house. Moreover, Mahomet and his companions, now shut up and almost besieged within a definite quarter of the city, were precluded from all attempts to spread their faith. Mahomet had secured his little company of followers, but cut off from the rest of the city his cause remained stationary, neither gaining nor losing adherents, during the years 617-619.

The suras of this period show some of the discouragement he felt at the time, but through them all beats a note of endurance and confidence: God is continually behind his cause, therefore that cause will prevail against all obstacles. Mahomet has become more familiar with the Jewish Scriptures, and many of the suras are recapitulations of the lives of Jewish heroes, especial preference being given to Abraham as mythical founder of his race, and to Lot as the typical example of one righteous man sent to warn the iniquitous. The style has certainly matured, and in so doing has lost much of its primal fire. It is still stirring and vibrant, but passages of almost bald narrative are interposed, shadows upon the shining floor of his original zeal. He has become increasingly reiterative, too,—a quality easily attained by those who have but one message, in this case a message of warning and exhortation, and are feverishly anxious to brand its urgency upon the hearts of their fellow-men.

Confined within so limited an area, his energy recoiled upon itself, and the despondency that so easily besets men of action when that necessity is denied them, overcame his mind. Only at the yearly pilgrimage was he able to gain a hearing from his Meccan brethren, and then, says the chronicler bitterly, "none would believe." The Hashim could not trade or intermarry with any outside their clan, and there seemed no chance of circumstances removing their disabilities. Mahomet's hopes of embracing all Mecca in his faith wavered and fled, until it seemed as if Allah no longer protected his chosen.

But after two years of negation and impotence, an end to the persecution of the Muslim was in sight, and in 619 the ban was removed. Legend has it that when the chiefs of the Kaaba went to look upon the document they found it devoured by ants, and took this as a sign of the displeasure of their gods. The ban was thus removed by supernatural agency when its prolongation would have meant final disaster for Mahomet. In the light of later knowledge it is evident that the removal of the ban was the result of the exertions of Abu Talib, and it was owing to his high reputation among the Kureisch that they pardoned his turbulent and blasphemous nephew. At the end of two years also, the Muslim were considerably weakened, both in staying powers and reputation. They were now allowed to go freely in the city, and the immediate prospect seemed certainly brighter for Mahomet when there fell the greatest blow that could have afflicted his sensitive spirit.

Khadijah, his companion and sustainer through so many troublous years, died in 619, having borne with him all his revilings and discouragements, his source of strength even when there appeared no prospect of the abatement of his hardships, much less for the success of his cause. Mahomet's grief was too profound for the passing shadow of it even to darken the pages of the Kuran. He paid her the compliment of silence; but her memory was continually with him, even when he had taken many fairer women to wife. Ayesha, in all the insolence of beauty, scoffed at Khadijah's age and lack of comeliness:

"Am I not dearer to thee than she was?"

"No, by Allah!" cried Mahomet; "for she believed when no one else believed."

It was her strength of character and sweetness of mind that impelled him to utter the amazing words—amazing for his time and environment, seventh-century Arabia—"women are the twin-halves of men."

But fortune or Allah had not finished the "strong affliction" whereby Mahomet was forced to cast off from his moorings and venture into strange and perilous seas. Five weeks after the death of his wife came the death of his uncle, Abu Talib. If the first had been a catastrophe affecting his courage and quietude of mind, this was calculated to crush both himself and his companions. Abu Talib was well loved by Mahomet, who manifested throughout his life the strongest capacity for friendship. But more important than the personal grief was the loss of the one man whose efforts bridged over the widening gulf between himself and the Kureisch. As such, his death was irreparable damage to Mahomet's safety from their hostilities.

Abu Lahab, it is true, touched a little by the sorrows crowding so thickly upon his nephew, protected him for a time, but very soon withdrew his support and joined the opposition. Ranged against Abu Lahab and Abu Jahl, with their influential following, and lacking the support hitherto provided by Abu Talib, Mahomet perceived that a crisis was fast approaching. His band was too numerous to be ignored or even tolerated by the Kureisch, but against such odds as Mecca's most powerful citizens, Mahomet was too wise to attempt to resist. There seemed no other way but the withdrawal of his little concourse to such place of safety as would enable them to strengthen themselves and prepare for the inevitable struggle for supremacy. No more conversions of importance had taken place since Omar's and Hamza's allegiance to Islam, and now three years had passed. Mahomet felt increasingly the need for their exodus from the city of his birth. It is not evident from the chroniclers that he had any definite political aims whatever when he first considered the plan of evacuation. His motive was simply to obtain peace in which he might worship in his own fashion, and win others to worship with him. With this idea in mind he cast about for a suitable resting-place for his small flock, and discovered what he imagined his goal in Taif, a village south-east of Mecca, upon the eastern slopes of Jhebel Kora.

Taif is situated on the fertile side of this mountain range, the side remote from the sea. It stands amid a wealth of gardens, and is renowned for its fruits and flowers. Thither in 620 Mahomet set out, filled with the knowledge of his invincible mission, strong in his power to conquer and persuade. Zeid, his slave and foster-child, was his only companion, and together they had resolved to convert Taif to the one true religion. But their adventure was doomed to failure, and though we have necessarily brief descriptions of it, all Mahomet's biographers naturally passing quickly over so painful a scene, there is sufficient evidence to show how really disastrous their venture proved.

The chief men of the city remained unconvinced, and at last the populace, in one of those blind furies that attack crowds at the sight of impotence, egged on the rabble to stone them. Chased from the city, sore, bleeding and despairing, Mahomet found shelter in one of the hill gardens of the locality. There he was solaced with fruit by some kindly owners of the place, and there he remained, meditating in profound dejection at his failure, but still with supreme trust in the support of his God.

"O Lord, I seek refuge in the light of Thy countenance;
It is Thine to cleanse away the darkness,
And to give peace both for this world and the next."

In this valley of Nakhla, too, so runs the tale, he was consoled by genii, who refreshed him, after the fashion of angels upholding the weary prophets in the wilderness. Mahomet was now in dire straits; he could not return to Mecca at once, because the object of his Taif journey was known; as Taif had spurned him, so he was forced to halt in Hira until he obtained the protection of Mutaim, an influential man in Mecca, and after some difficulty made his way back to the city, discredited and solitary, except for his former followers. For some months he rested in obscurity and contempt at Mecca, gaining none to his cause, but still filled with the fervent conviction of his future triumph, which neither wavered nor faltered. The divine fire which upheld him during the period of his violent persecution burned within his soul, and never was his steadfastness of character and faith in himself and his mission more fully manifested than during these despondent months.

He now began to seek in greater measure the society of women, although the consuming sexual life of his later years had hardly awakened. While Khadijah was with him he remained faithful to her, but her bright presence once withdrawn, he was impelled by a kind of impassioned seeking to the quest for her substitute, and not finding it in one woman, to continue his search among others. He now married Sawda, a nonentity with a certain physical charm but no personality, and sued for the hand of Ayesha, the small daughter of Abu Bekr.

Mahomet at this time was not blessed with many riches. His frugal, anxious life led him to perform many small duties of his household for himself. His food was coarse and often scanty, and he lived among his followers as one of themselves. It is no small tribute to his singleness of mind and lofty character that in the "dreary intercourse of daily life," lived in that primitive, communal fashion, which admits of no illusions and scarcely any secrets, he retained by the force of personality the reverence of the faithful, and ever in this hour of defeat and negation remained their leader and lord—the symbol, in fact, of their loyalty to Allah, and their supreme belief in his guidance and care.

CHAPTER VII

THE CHOSEN CITY

Medina, city of exile and despairing beginnings, destined to achieve glory by difficult ways, only to be eclipsed finally by its mightier neighbour and mistress, became, rather by chance than by design, the scene of Mahomet's struggles for temporal power and his ruthless wielding of the sword for God and Islam. The city lies north-east of Mecca, on the opposite side of the mountain spur that skirts the eastern boundary. Always weakly peopled, it remained from immemorial time an arena of strife, for it was on the borderland, the boundary of several tribes, and was far enough north for the outer waves of Syrian disturbances to fling their varying tides upon its shores—a meagre city, always fiercely at civil warfare, impotent, unfertile.

In the dark days of Judaea's humiliation at the hands of Titus, two Jewish tribes, the Kainukua and the Koreitza, outcast and desolate, even as they had been warned in their time of dominion, lighted upon Medina in desperate search for a dwelling-place and a respite from persecution, and forthwith took possession of the little hill-girt town. They settled there, driving out or conciliating the former inhabitants, until in the fourth century their tenuous prosperity was disturbed by the inroads of two Bedouin tribes, the Beni Aus and the Beni Khazraj. The desert was wide, and these tribes were familiar with its manifold opportunities and devious ways. Against such a foe, who swooped down suddenly upon the city, plundered and then escaped into the limitless unknown, the Jews had no chance of reprisal.

Before long the Beni Aus and Khazraj had subjugated the Jewish communities, and their dominion in Medina was only weakened by their devastating quarrels among themselves. The city therefore offered a peculiar opening for the teaching of Islam within it. Its religious life indeed was varied and chaotic. Jews, Arabian idolaters, immigrants from Christian Syria, torn by schisms, thronged its public places, and this confusion of faiths sharpened the religious and debating instincts of its people. The ground was thus broken up for the reception of the new creed of one God and of his messenger, who had already divided Mecca into believers and heretics, and who was spoken of in the city with that awe that attaches itself to distant marvels.

Intercourse with Mecca was chiefly carried on at the time of the yearly Pilgrimage; the Greater Pilgrimage, only undertaken during Dzul Hijj, corresponding then to our March, and in Dzul Hijj, 620, came a band of strangers over the hills, along the toilsome caravan route to the Kaaba, the goal of their intentions, the shrine of all their prayers. They performed all the necessary ceremonies at Mecca, and were proceeding to Mina, a small valley just east of Mecca, for the completion of their sacred duties, when they were accosted by Mahomet.

The Prophet was despondent and sceptical of his power to persuade, though his belief in Allah's might never wavered. He had failed so far to produce any decisive impression upon the Meccan people, but might there not be another town in Arabia which would receive his message? The little band of pilgrims seemed to him sent in answer to his self-distrust, and his failure at Taif as eclipsed by this sudden success. The caravan returned to its native city, and there remained little for Mahomet to do except to wait for the arrival of next year's pilgrims, and to keep shining and ambient the flame of his religious fervour. He remained in Mecca virtually on sufferance, and rapidly recognised the uselessness of attempting any further conversions. His hopes were now definitely set on Medina, and to this end he seems to devoted himself more than ever to the perusal and interpretation of the Jewish scriptures.

The portion of the Kuran written at this time contains little else than Bible stories told and retold to the point of weariness. Lot, of course, is the characteristic figure; but we also have the life stories of Abraham, Moses, Jonah, Joseph, and many others. The style has suffered a marked diminution in poetic qualities. It has become reiterative and even laboured. He continues his practice of alluding to current events, which at Medina he was to pursue to the extent of making the Kuran a kind of spasmodic history of his time, as well as an elementary text-book of law and morality. In one of the suras—"The Cow"—Mahomet makes first mention of that comfortable doctrine of "cancelling," by which later verses of the Kuran cancel all previous revelations dealing with the same subject if these prove contradictory: "Whatever verses we cancel or cause thee to forget, we bring a better or its like; knowest thou not that God hath power over all things?"

There is not much record in the Kuran of the influence of Christian thought upon Islam. We have a few stories of Elizabeth and Mary, and scattered allusions to the despised "Prophet of the Jews." But the great body of Christian thought, its central dogmas of Incarnation and Redemption, passed Mahomet entirely by, for his mind was practical and not speculative, and indeed to himself no less than to his followers the fundamentals of Christianity were of necessity too philosophic to be realised with any intensity of belief. The Christian virtues of meekness and resignation, too, might be respected in the abstract—passages in the Kuran and tradition assure us they were—but they were so utterly antagonistic to the fierce, free nature of the Arab that they never entered into his religious life. Mahomet revered the Founder of Christianity, and placed Him with John in the second Heaven of his Immortals, but though He is secure among the teachers of the world, He can never compete with the omnipotence and glory of the Prophet.

During the period of Mahomet's life immediately preceding his departure to Medina, we have his personal appearance described in detail by Ali. He is a man of medium stature, with a magnificent head and a thick, flowing beard. His eyes were black and ardent, his jaw firm but not prominent. He looked an upstanding man of open countenance, benignant and powerful, bearing between his shoulders the sign of his divine mission. He had great patience, says Ali, and "in nowise despised the poor for their poverty, nor honoured the rich for their possessions. Nor if any took him by the hand to salute him was he the first to relinquish his grasp."

He lived openly among his disciples, holding frequent converse with them, mending his own clothes and even shoes, a frugal liver and a fervent preacher of the flaming faith within him. He became at this time betrothed to Ayesha, the splendid woman, now just a merry child, who was to keep her reigning place in his affections until the end of his life. Daughter of Abu Bekr, she united in herself for Mahomet both policy and attractiveness, for by this betrothal he became of blood-kin with Abu Bekr, and thereby strengthened his friend's allegiance. The union marks the inauguration of his policy of marriage alliances by which he bound the supporters of his Faith more closely to him, either through his own marriage with their daughters, or the bestowal of his offspring upon them.

Ayesha was lovely and imperious, with a luxurious but shrewd nature, and her counsel was always sought by Mahomet. Other women appeared frequently like comets in his sky, flamed for a little into brightness and disappeared into conjugal obscurity, but Ayesha's star remained fixed, even if it was transitorily eclipsed by the brilliance of a new-comer. Sexual relations held for Mahomet towards the end of his life a peculiar potency, born of his intense energetic nature. He sought the society of woman because of the mental clarity that for him followed any expression of emotion. He was one of those men who must express—the artist, in fact; but an artist who used the medium of action, not that of literature, painting, or music. "Poète, il ne connut que la poésie d'action," and like Napoleon, his introspection was completely overshadowed by his consuming energy. Therefore emotion was to him unconsciously the means by which this immortal energy of mind could be conserved, and he used it unsparingly.

Ayesha has revealed for us the most intimate details of Mahomet's life, and it is due to her that later traditions are enabled to represent him as a man among men. He appears to us fierce and subtle, by turns impetuous and calculating, a man who never missed an opportunity, and gauged exactly the efforts needed to compass any intention. To him "every fortress had its key, and every man his price." He was as keen a politician us he was a religious reformer, but before all he paid homage to the sword, prime artificer in his career of conquest. But in those confidently intimate traditions handed down to us from his immediate entourage, and especially from Ayesha, we find him alternately passionate and gentle, wearing his power with conscious authority, mild in his treatment of the poor, terrible to his enemies, autocratic, intolerant, with a strange magnetism that bound men to him. The mystery enveloping great men even in their lifetime, among primitive races, creeps down in these documents to hide much of his personality from us, but his works proclaim his energy and tireless organising powers, even if the mythical, allegoric element predominates in the earlier traditions. The man who undertook and achieved the gigantic task of organising a new social and political as well as religious order may be justly credited with calling forth and centering in himself the vivid imaginations of that most credulous age.

The year 620-621 passed chiefly in expectation of the Greater Pilgrimage, when the disciples from Medina were to come to report progress and to confirm their faith. The momentous time arrived, and Mahomet went almost fearfully to meet the nucleus of his future kingdom in Acaba, a valley near Mina. But his fears were groundless, for the little party had been faithful to their leader, and had also increased their numbers.

They met in secret, and we may picture them a little diffident in so strange a place, ever expectant of the swift descent of the Kureisch and their own annihilation. Withal they were enthusiastic and confident of their leader. One is irresistibly reminded, in reading of this meeting, of that little outcast band from Judea which ultimately prevailed over Cæsar Imperator through its mighty quality of faith. The accredited words of the first pledge given at Acaba are traditionally extant; they combine curiously religious, moral, and social covenants, and assert even at that early stage the headship of the Prophet over his servants:

"We will not worship any but God; we will not steal, neither will we commit adultery nor kill our children; we will not slander in any wise, nor will we disobey the Prophet in anything that is right."

The converts then departed to their native city, for Mahomet did not deem the time yet ripe enough for migration thither. He possessed the difficult art of waiting until the effectual time should arrive, and there is no doubt that by now he had formed definite plans to set up his rule in Medina when there should be sufficient supporters there to guarantee his success. Musab, a Meccan convert of some learning, was deputed to accompany the Medinan citizens to their city and give instruction therein to all who were willing to study the Muslim creed.

For yet another year Mahomet was to possess his soul in patience, but it was with feelings of far greater confidence that he awaited the passing of time. More than ever he became sure of the guiding hand of Allah, that pointed indisputably to the stranger city as the goal of his strivings. This city held a goodly proportion of Jews, therefore the connection between his faith and that of Judaism must be continually emphasised.

We have seen how large a space Jewish legend and history fill in the contemporary suras of the Kuran, and Mahomet's friendship with Israel increased noticeably during his last two years at Mecca. He paid them the honour of taking Jerusalem as his Kibla, or Holy Place, to which all

Believers turn in prayer, and the starting-place for his immortal Midnight Journey was the Sacred City encompassing the Temple of the Lord.

No account of this journey appears except in the traditions crystallized by Al Bokharil, but there is one short mention of it in the Kuran, Sura xviii.

"Glory be to him who carried his servant by night from the sacred temple of Mecca to the temple that is more remote, i.e. Jerusalem."

The vision, however, looms so large in his followers' minds, and exercised so profound an influence over their regard for Mahomet, that it throws some light, upon the measure of his ascendancy during his last years at Mecca, and establishes beyond dispute the inspired character of his Prophetship in the imaginations of the few Believers. There have been solemn and wordy disputes by theologians as to whether he made the journey in the flesh, or whether his spirit alone crossed the dread portals dividing our night from the celestial day.

He was lying in the Kaaba, so runs the legend, when the Angel of the Lord appeared to him, and after having purged his heart of all sin, carried him to the Temple at Jerusalem. He penetrated its sacred enclosure and saw the beast Borak, "greater than ass, smaller than mule," and was told to mount. The Faithful still show the spot at Jerusalem where his steed's hoof marked the ground as he spurned it with flying feet. With Gabriel by his side, mounted on a beast mighty in strength, Mahomet scaled the appalling spaces and came at last to the outer Heaven, before the gate that guards the celestial realms. The angel knocked upon the brazen doors and a voice within cried:

"Who art thou, and who is with thee?"

"I am Gabriel," came the answer, "and this is Mahomet."

And behold, the brazen gates that may not be unclosed for mortal man were flung wide, and Mahomet entered alone with the angel. He penetrated to the first Heaven and saw Adam, who interrogated him in the same words, and received the same reply. And all the heavenly hierarchies, even unto the seventh Heaven, John and Jesus, Joseph, Enoch, Aaron, Moses, Abraham, acknowledged Mahomet in the same words, until the two came to "the tree called Sedrat," beyond which no man may pass and live, whose fruits are shining serpents, and whose leaves are great beasts, round which flow four rivers, the Nile and the Euphrates guarding it without, and within these the celestial streams that water Paradise, too wondrous for a name.

Awed but undaunted, Mahomet passed alone beyond the sacred tree, for even the Angel could not bear any longer so fierce a glory, and came to Al-M'amur, even the Hall of Heavenly Audience, where are seventy thousand angels. He mounted the steps of the throne between their serried ranks, until at the touch of Allah's awful hand he stopped and felt its icy coldness penetrate to his heart. He was given milk, wine, or honey to drink, and he chose milk.

"Hadst thou chosen honey, O Mahomet," said Allah, "all thy people would be saved, now only a part shall find perfection."

And Mahomet was troubled.

"Bid my people pray to Me fifty times a day."

At the resistless mandate Mahomet turned and retraced his steps to the seventh Heaven, where dwelt Abraham.

"The people of the earth will be in nowise constrained to pray fifty times a day. Return thou and beg that the number be lessened."

So Mahomet returned again and again at Abraham's command, until he had reduced the number to five, which the father of his people considered was sufficient burden for his feeble subjects to bear. Wherefore the five periods set apart for prayer in the Muslim faith are proportionately sacred, and with this divine mandate the vision ceased.

With his hopes now set on founding an earthly dominion with the help of Allah, he had perforce to consider the political situation, and to mature his policy for dealing with it as soon as events proved favourable. The achievements of the Persians on the Greek frontier had already attracted his attention in 616; there is an allusion to the battle and the Greek defeat in the Kuran, and a vague prophecy of their ultimate success, for Mahomet was in sympathy with the Greek Empire, seeing that, from the point of view of Arabia, it was the less formidable enemy.

But really the events of such outlying territories only troubled him in regard to Medina, for his whole thoughts were centred now upon the chosen city of his dreams. His followers became less aggressive in Mecca when they knew that the Prophet had the nucleus of a new colony in another city. Persecution within Mecca therefore died down considerably, and the period is one of pause upon either side, the Kureisch watching to see what the next move was to be, Mahomet carefully and secretly maturing his plans.

During this year there fell a drought upon Mecca, followed by a famine, which the devout attributed directly to divine anger at the rejection of the Prophet's heavenly message, and which Mahomet interpreted as the punishment of God, and this doubtless added to the sum of reasons which impelled him to relinquish his native town.

From this time until the Hegira, or Flight from the City, events in the world of action move but slowly for Mahomet. He was careful not to excite undue suspicion among the Kureisch, and we can imagine him silent and preoccupied, fulfilling his duties among them, visiting the Kaaba, and mingling somewhat coldly with their daily life. Still keeping his purpose immutable, he sought to strengthen the faith of his followers for the trials he knew must come. The Kuran thus became more important as the mouthpiece of his exhortations. The suras of this time resound with words of encouragement and confidence. He is about to become the leader of a perilous venture in honour of God. The reflex of the expectancy in the hearts of the Muslim may be traced in his messages to them. Their whole world, as it were, waited breathless, quiet, and tense for the record of the year's achievements in Medina, and for the time appointed by God. But how far their leader's actions were the result of painstaking calculations, an insight into the qualities and energies of men, a prevision startling in its range and accuracy, they never suspected; but, serene in their confidence, they held their magnificent faith in the divine guidance and in the inspiration of their Prophet.

CHAPTER VIII

THE FLIGHT TO MEDINA

"Knowest thou not that the dominion of the Heavens and of the Earth is God's? and that ye have neither patron nor helper save God?"—*The Kuran.*

The expectancy which burned like revivifying fire in the hearts of the Meccan Muslim, kindled and nourished by their leader himself, was to culminate at the time of the yearly pilgrimage in 622. In that month came the great concourse of pilgrims from Yathreb to Mecca, among them seventy of the "Faithful" who had received the faith at Medina, headed by their teacher Musab and strengthened by the knowledge that they were before long to stand face to face with their Prophet.

Musab had reported to Mahomet the success of his mission in the city, and had prepared him for the advent of the little band of followers secured for Islam. Secrecy was essential, for the Muslim from Medina were in heart strangers among their own people, in such a precarious situation that any treachery would have meant their utter annihilation, if not at the hands of their countrymen, who would doubtless throw in their lot with the stronger, certainly at the hands of the Kureisch, the implacable foes of Islam, in whose territory they fearfully were. The rites of pilgrimage were accordingly performed faithfully, though many breathed more freely as they departed for the last ceremony at Mina. All was now completed, and the Medinan party prepared to return, when Mahomet summoned the Faithful by night to the old meeting-place in the gloomy valley of Akaba.

About seventy men and two women of both Medinan tribes, the Beni Khazraj and the Beni Aus, assembled thus in that barren place, under the brilliant night skies of Arabia, to pledge themselves anew to an unseen, untried God and to the service of his Prophet, who as yet counted but few among his followers, and whose word carried no weight with the great ones of their world.

To this meeting Mahomet brought Abbas, his uncle, younger son of Abd-al-Muttalib, a weak and insignificant character, who had endeared himself to Mahomet chiefly because of his doglike devotion. He was not a convert, but he revered his energetic nephew too highly and was also too greatly in awe of him to imagine such a thing as treachery. He was in part a guarantee to the Khazraj of Mahomet's good faith, in part an asset for him against the Kureisch, for his family were still influential in Mecca.

The two made their way from the city unaccompanied, by steep and stony ways, until they came to Akaba, and Mahomet saw awaiting him that concourse summoned by his persistence and tireless faith—a concourse part of himself, almost his own child, upon which all his hopes were now set. Coming thus into that circle of faces, illumined dimly by the torches, which prudence even now urged them to extinguish, he could not but feel some foreshadowing of the mighty future that awaited this little gathering, as yet impotent and tremulous, but bearing within itself the seeds of that loyalty and courage that were to spread "the Faith" over half the world.

When the greetings were over, Abbas stepped forward and spoke, while the lines of dark faces closed around him in earnest scrutiny.

"Ye men of the Beni Khazraj, this my kinsmen dwelleth amongst us in honour and safety; his clan will defend him, but he preferreth to seek protection from you. Wherefore, ye Khazraj, consider the matter well and count the cost."

Then answered Bara, who stood for them in position of Chief:

"We have listened to your words. Our resolution is unshaken. Our lives are at the Prophet's service. It is now for him to speak."

Mahomet stepped forward into the circle of their glances, and with the solemnity of the occasion urgent within him recited to them verses of the Kuran, whose fire and eloquence kindled those passionate souls into an enthusiasm glowing with a sombre resolve, and prompted them to stake all upon their enterprise. At the end of those tumultuous words he assured them that he would be content if they would pledge themselves to defend him.

"And if we die in thy defence, what reward have we?"

"Paradise!" replied Mahomet, exalted, raising his hand in token of his belief in Allah and the certitude of his cause.

Then arose a murmur deep and long, the protestation of loyalty that threatened to rise into triumphant acclamation, but Abbas, the fearful of the party, stayed them in dread of spies. So the tumult died down, and Bara, taking upon himself the authority of his fellows, stretched forth his hand to Mahomet, and with their clasping the Second Pledge of the Akaba was sealed. They broke up swiftly, dreading to prolong their meeting, for danger was all around them and the air heavy with suspected treacheries.

And their apprehension was not groundless, for the Kureisch had heard of their assembly through some secret messenger, though not until the Medinan caravan with its concourse of the Faithful and the Unbelievers was well on its homeward way across the dreary desert paths which lead to Mecca from Medina. Their wrath was intense, and in fury they pursued it; but either they were ignorant as to which road the party had taken, or the Medinans eluded them by greater speed, for they returned disconsolate from the pursuit, having only succeeded in finding two luckless men, one of whom escaped, but the other, Sa'd ibn Obada, was dragged back to Mecca and subjected to much brutality before he ultimately made his escape to his native city.

The Kureisch were not content with attempting reprisals against Medina, or possibly they were enraged because they had effected so little, for they recommenced the persecution of Islam at Mecca with much violence. From March until April they harassed the Believers in their city, imposing restrictions upon them, and in many cases inflicting bodily harm upon Mahomet's unfortunate and now defenceless followers. The renewed persecution doubtless gave an added impetus to the Prophet's resolve to quit Mecca.

Indeed, the time was fully ripe, and with the prescience that continually characterised him in his role of leader of a religious state, he felt that now the ground was prepared at Medina, emigration of the Muslim from Mecca could not fail to be advantageous to him.

The command was given in April 622, and found immediate popularity, except with a few malcontents who had large interests in their native city. Then began the slow removal of a whole colony. The families of Abu Talib's quarter of Mecca tranquilly forsook their birthplace in orderly groups, taking with them their household treasures, until the neighbourhood showed tenantless houses falling into the swift decay accompanying neglect in such a climate, barricaded doors and gaping windows, filled only with an immense feeling of desolation and the blankness which overtakes a city when its humanity has deputed to another abiding place. Weeds grew in the deserted streets, and over all lay a fine film of dust, the almost impalpable effort of the desert to merge once more into itself the territory wrung from it by human will.

The effect of this emigration upon the Kureisch can hardly be estimated. They were amazed and helpless before it; for with their wrath hot against Mahomet, it was as if their antagonist had melted into insubstantial vapours to leave them enraged and breathless, pursuing a phantom continually elusive. So silent was the emigration that they were only made aware of it when the quarter was almost deserted. Scattered groups of travellers journeying along the desert tracks had evoked no hostilities, and no treachery broke the loyalty to Islam at Mecca. The Kureisch were indeed outwitted, and only became conscious of the subtleties of their antagonist when his plan was accomplished.

But in spite of the seemingly favourable situation, the leader tarried because "the Lord had not as yet given him command to emigrate." The very natural hesitation of Mahomet is only characteristic of him. He knew very well what issues were at stake, and was not anxious to burn his boats rashly; indeed, he bore upon his shoulders at this time all the responsibility of the future of his little flock, who so confidently resigned their fortunes into his hands. If his scheme at Medina should fail, he knew that nothing would save him from Kureischite fury, and he also felt great reluctance in leaving Mecca himself, for at that time it could not but mean the knell of his hopes of gaining his native city to his creed. He must have foreseen his establishment of power in Medina, and possibly he had visions of its extension to neighbouring tribes, but he could not have foreseen the humiliation of his native city at his feet, glad at last to receive the faith of one whom she now regarded as the sovereign potentate of Arabian territory.

And with their friend and guide remained Abu Bekr and Ali—Abu Bekr because he would not leave his companion in prayer and persecution, and Ali because his valour and enthusiasm made him a protector against possible attacks. Here was the opportunity for the Kureisch. They knew the extent of the emigration, and that Abu Bekr and Ali were the only Muslim of importance left except the Prophet. They determined to make one last attempt to coerce into submission this fantastic but resolute leader, who possessed in supreme measure the power of winning the faith and devotion of men.

Tradition has it that Mahomet's assassination was definitely planned, and Mahomet assuredly thought so too, when he discovered that a man from each tribe had been chosen to visit his home at night. The motive can hardly have been assassination, but doubtless the chiefs were prepared to take rather strong measures to restrain Mahomet, and this action finally decided the Prophet that delay was dangerous.

At this crisis in his fortunes he had two staunch helpers, who did not hesitate to risk their lives in his service, and with them he anticipated his foes. Ali was chosen to represent his beloved master before the menaces of the Kureisch. Mahomet put him into his own bed and arrayed him in his sacred green mantle; then, as legend has it, taking a handful of dust, he recited the sura "Ya Sin," which he himself reverenced as "the heart of the Kuran," and scattering the dust abroad, he called down confusion upon the heads of the Unbelievers. With Abu Bekr he then fled swiftly and silently from the city and made his way unseen to the cave of Thaur, a few miles outside its boundaries.

Around the cave of Thaur cluster as many and as beautiful legends as surround the stable at Bethlehem. The wild pigeons flew out and in unharmed, screening the Prophet by their untroubled presence from the searchings of the Kureisch, and a thorn tree spread her branches across the mouth of the cave supporting a spider's frail and glistening web, which was renewed whenever a friend visited the two prisoners to bring food and tidings.

Here Mahomet and Abu Bekr, henceforward known as the "Second of Two," remained until the fierceness of the pursuit slackened. Asma, Abu Bekr's daughter, brought them food at sundown, and what news she could glean from the rumours that were abroad, and from the lips of Ali. There was very real danger of their surprise and capture, but once more Mahomet's magnificent faith in God and his cause never wavered. Abu Bekr was afraid for his master:

"We are but two, and if the Kureisch find us unarmed, what chance have we?"

"We are but two," replied Mahomet, "but God is in the midst a third."

He looked unflinchingly to Allah for succour and protection, and his faith was justified. His thanksgiving is contained in the Kuran: "God assisted your Prophet formerly, when the Unbelievers drove him forth in company with a second only; when they two were in the cave; when the Prophet said to his companion, 'Be not distressed; verily God is with us.' And God sent down his tranquillity upon him and strengthened him with hosts ye saw not, and made the word of those who believed not the abased, and the word of God was the exalted."

At the end of three days the Kureischite search abated, and that night Mahomet and Abu Bekr decided to leave the cave. Two camels were brought, and food loaded upon them by Asma and her servants. The fastenings were not long enough to tie on the food wallet; wherefore Asma tore her girdle in two and bound them round it, so that she is known to this day among the Faithful as "She of Two Shreds." After a prayer to Allah in thanks for their safety, Mahomet and Abu Bekr mounted the camels and sallied forth to meet what unknown destiny should await them on the road to Medina. They rapidly gained the sea-coast near Asfan in comparative safety, secure from the attacks of the Kureisch, who would not pursue their quarry so far into a strange country.

The Kureisch had indeed considerably abated their anger against Mahomet. He was now safely out of their midst, and possibly they thought themselves well rid of a man whose only object, from their point of view, was to stir up strife, and they felt that any resentment against either himself or his kin would be unnecessary and not worth their pains. With remarkable tolerance for so revengeful an age, they left the families of Mahomet and Abu Bekr quite free from molestation, nor did they offer any opposition to Ali when they found he had successfully foiled them, and he made his way out of the city three days after his leader had quitted it.

Mahomet and Abu Bekr journeyed on, two pilgrims making their way, solitary but unappalled, to a strange city, whose temper and disposition they but faintly understood. But evidences as to its friendliness were not wanting, and these were renewed when Abu Bekr's cousin, a previous emigrant to Medina, met them half-way and declared that the city waited in joy and expectation for the coming of its Prophet. After some days they crossed the valley of Akik in extreme heat, and came at last to Coba, an outlying suburb at Medina, where, weary and apprehensive, Mahomet rested for a while, prudently desiring that his welcome at Medina might be assured before he ventured into its confines.

His entry into Coba savoured of a triumphal procession; the people thronged around his camel shouting, "The Prophet; he is come!" mingling their cries with homage and wondering awe, that the divine servant of whom they had heard so much should appear to them in so human a guise, a man among them, verily one of themselves. Mahomet's camel stopped at the house of Omm Kolthum, and there he elected to abide during his stay in Coba, for he possessed throughout his life a reverence for the instinct in animals that characterises the Eastern races of all time. There, dismounting, he addressed the people, bidding them be of good cheer, and giving them thanks for their joyous welcome:

"Ye people, show your joy by giving your neighbours the salvation of peace; send portions to the poor; bind close the ties of kinship, and offer up your prayers whilst others sleep. Thus shall ye enter Paradise in peace."

For four days Mahomet dwelt in Coba, where he had encountered unfailing support and friendship, and there was joined by Ali. His memories of Coba were always grateful, for at the outset of his doubtful and even dangerous enterprise he had received a good augury. Before he set out to Medina he laid the foundations of the Mosque at Coba, where the Faithful would be enabled to pray according to their fashion, undisturbed and beneath the favour of Allah, and decreed that Friday was to be set apart as a special day of prayer, when addresses were to be given at the Mosque and the doctrines of Islam expounded.

Even as early as this Mahomet felt the mantle of sovereignty descending upon him, for we hear now of the first of those ordinances or decrees by which in later times he rules the lives and actions of his subjects to the last detail. Clearly he perceived himself a leader among men, who had it within his power to build up a community following his own dictates, which might by consolidation even rival those already existent in Arabia. He was taking command of a weak and factious city, and he realised that in his hands lay its prosperity or downfall; he was, in fact, the arbiter of its fate and of the fate of his colleagues who had dared all with him.

But he could not stay long in Coba, while the final assay upon the Medinans remained to be undertaken, and so we find him on the fourth day of his sojourn making preparations for the entry into the city. It was undertaken with some confidence of success from the messages already sent to Coba, and proved as triumphal an entry as his former one. The populace awaited him in expectation and reverence, and hailed him as their Prophet, the mighty leader who had come to their deliverance. They surrounded his camel Al-Caswa, and the camels of his followers, and when Al-Caswa stopped outside the house of Abu Ayub, Mahomet once more received the beast's augury and sojourned there until the building of the Mosque. As Al-Caswa entered the paved courtyard, Mahomet dismounted to receive the allegiance of Abu Ayub and his household; then, turning to the people, he greeted them with words of good cheer and encouragement, and they responded with acclamations.

For seven months the Prophet lodged in the house of Abu Ayub, and he bought the yard where Al-Caswa halted as a token of his first entry into Medina, and a remembrance in later years of his abiding place during the difficult time of his inception. The decisive step had been taken. The die was now cast. It was as if the little fleet of human souls had finally cast its moorings and ventured into the unpathed waters of temporal dominion under the command of one whose skill in pilotage was as yet unknown. Many changes became necessary in the conduct of the enterprise, of which not the least was the change of attitude between the leader and his followers. Mahomet, heretofore religious visionary and teacher, became the temporal head of a community, and in time the leader of a political State. The changed aspect of his mission can never be over-emphasised, for it altered the tenor of his thoughts and the progress of his words. All the poetry and fire informing the early pages of the Kuran departs with his reception at Medina, except for occasional flashes that illumine the chronicle of detailed ordinances that the Book has now become.

This apparent death of poetic energy had crept gradually over the Kuran, helped on by the controversial character of the last two Meccan periods, when he attempted the conciliation of the Jewish element within Arabia with that long-sightedness which already discerned Medina as his possible refuge. In reality the whole energy of his nature was transmuted from his words to his actions and therein he found his fitting sphere, for he was essentially the doer, one whose works are the expression of his secret, whose personality, in fact, is only gauged by his deeds. As a result of his political leadership, the despotism of his nature, inherent in his conception of God, inevitably revealed itself; he had postulated a Being who held mankind in the hollow of his hand, whose decrees were absolute among his subjects; now that he was to found an earthly kingdom under the guidance of Allah, the majesty of divine despotism overshadowed its Prophet, and enabled him to impose upon a willing people the same obedience to authority which fostered the military idea.

We must perforce believe in Mahomet's good faith. There is a tendency in modern times to think of him as a man who knowingly played upon the credulity of his followers to establish a sovereignty whereof he should be head. But no student of psychology can support this conception of the Prophet of Islam. There is a subtle *rapprochement* between leader and people in all great movements that divines instinctively any imposture. Mahomet used and moulded men by reason of his faith in his own creed. The establishment of the worship of Allah brought in its train the aggrandisement of his Prophet, but it was not achieved by profanation of the source whence his greatness came.

Mahomet is the last of those leaders who win both the religious devotion and the political trust of his followers. He wrought out his sovereignty perforce and created his own *milieu*; but more than all, he diffused around him the tradition of loyalty to one God and one state with sword for artificer, which outlived its creator through centuries of Arabian prosperity. Stone by slow stone his empire was built up, an edifice owing its contour to his complete grasp of detail and his dauntless energy. The last days at Mecca had shown him a careful schemer, the early days at Medina proved his capacity as leader and his skill in organisation and government.

CHAPTER IX

THE CONSOLIDATION OF POWER

"The Infidels, moreover, will say: Thou art not sent of God. Say: God is witness enough betwixt me and you, and whoever hath knowledge of the Book."—*The Kuran.*

Mahomet, now established at Medina, at once began that careful planning of the lives of his followers and the ceaseless fostering of his own ideas within them that endeared him to the Believers as leader and lord, and enabled him in time to prosecute his designs against his opponents with a confidence in their faith and loyalty.

His grasp of detail was wonderful; without haste and without coercion he subdued the turbulent factions within Medina, and his own perfervid followers to discipline as despotic as it was salutary; Mahomet became what circumstances made him; by reason of his mighty gift of moulding those men and forces that came his way, he impressed his personality upon his age; but the material fashioning of his energy, the flower of his creative art, drew its formative sustenance from the soil of his surroundings. The time for admonition, with the voice of one crying in the wilderness, the time for praise and poesy, for the expression of that rapt immortal passion filling his mind as he contemplated God, all these were past, and had become but a lingering brightness upon the stormy urgency of his later life.

Now his flock demanded from him organisation, leadership, political and social prevision. Therefore the full force of his nature is revealed to us not so much as heretofore in the Kuran, but rather in his institutions and ordinances, his enmities and conciliations. He has become not only the Prophet, but the Lawgiver, the Statesman, almost the King.

His first act, after his establishment in the house of Abu Ayub, was the joining together in brotherhood of the Muhajerim and Ansar. These were two distinct entities within Medina; the Muhajerim (refugees) had either accompanied their master from Mecca or had emigrated previously; the Ansar (helpers) comprised all the converts to Islam within the city itself. These parties were now joined in a close bond, each individual taking another of the opposite party into brotherhood with himself, to be accorded the rights and privileges of kinship. Mahomet took as his brother Ali, who became indeed not only his kinsman, but his military commander and chief of staff. The wisdom of this arrangement, which lasted about a year and a half—until, in fact, its usefulness was outworn by the union of both the Medinan tribes under his leadership —was immediate and far-reaching. It enabled Mahomet to keep a close surveillance over the Medinan converts, who might possibly recant when they became aware of the hazards involved in partnership with the Muslim. It also gave a coherence to the two parties and allowed the Muhajerim some foothold in an alien city, not as yet unanimously friendly. And the Muhajerim had need of all the kindliness and help they could obtain, for the first six months in Medina were trying both to their health and endurance, so that many repented their venture and would have returned if the Ansar had not come forward with ministrations and gifts, and also if their chances of reaching Mecca alive had not been so precarious.

The climate at Medina is damp and variable. Hot days alternate with cold nights, and in winter there is almost continuous rain. The Meccans, used to the dry, hot days and nights of their native city, where but little rain fell, and even that became absorbed immediately in the parched ground, endured much discomfort, even pain, before becoming acclimatised. Fever broke out amongst them, and it was some months before the epidemic was stayed with the primitive medical skill at their command.

Nevertheless, in spite of their weakness and the difficulties of their position, in these first seven months the Mosque of Mahomet was built Legend says that the Prophet himself took a share in the work, carrying stones and tools with the humblest of his followers, and we can well believe that he did not look on at the labour of his fellow-believers, and that his consuming zeal prompted him to forward, in whatever way was necessary, the work lying to his hand.

The Medinan Mosque, built with fervent hearts and anxious prayers by the Muslim and their leader, contains the embryo of all the later masterpieces of Arabian architecture—that art unique and splendid, which developed with the Islamic spirit until it culminated in the glorious temple at Delhi, whose exponents have given to the world the palaces of southern Spain, the mysterious, remote beauty of ancient Granada. In its embryo minarets and domes, its slender arches and delicate traceries, it expressed the latent poetry in the heart of Islam which the claims of Allah and the fiercely jealous worship of him had hitherto obscured; for like Jahweh of old, Allah was an exacting spirit, who suffered no emotion but worship to be lord of his people's hearts.

The Mosque was square in design, made of stone and brick, and wrought with the best skill of which they were capable. The Kibla, or direction of prayer, was towards Jerusalem, symbolic of Mahomet's desire to propitiate the Jews, and finally to unite them with his own people in a community with himself as temporal head. Opposite this was the Bab Rahmah, the Gate of Mercy, and general entrance to the holy place. Ranged round the outer wall of the Mosque were houses for the Prophet's wives and daughters, little stone buildings, of two or three rooms, almost huts, where Mahomet's household had its home—Rockeya, his daughter, and Othman, her husband; Fatima and Ali, Sawda and Ayesha, soon to be his girl-bride, and who even now showed exceeding loveliness and force of character.

Mahomet himself had no separate house, but dwelt with each of his wives in turn, favouring Ayesha most, and as his harem increased a house was added for each wife, so that his entourage was continually near him and under his surveillance. On the north side the ground was open, and there the poorer followers of Mahomet gathered, living upon the never-failing hospitality of the East and its ready generosity in the necessities of life.

As soon as the Mosque was built, organised religious life at Medina came into being. A daily service was instituted in the Mosque itself, and the heaven-sent command to prayer five times a day for every Muslim was enforced. Five times in every turn of the world Allah receives his supplicatory incense; at dawn, at noon, in the afternoon, at sunset, and at night the Muslim renders his due reverence and praise to the lord of his welfare, thanking Allah, his supreme guide and votary, for the gift of the Prophet, guide and protector of the Faithful. Lustration before prayer was instituted as symbolic of the Believers' purification of heart before entering the presence of God, and provision for the ceremony made inside the Mosque. The public service on Friday, instituted at Coba, was continued at Medina, and consisted chiefly of a sermon given by Mahomet from a pulpit, erected inside the Mosque, whose sanctity was proverbial and unassailed. Thus the seed was sown of a corporate religious life, the embryo from which the Arabian military organisation, its polity, even its social system, were to spring.

In spite of the increasing numbers of the Ansar, there still remained a party in Medina, "the Disaffected," who had not as yet accepted the Prophet or his creed. Over these Mahomet exercised a strict surveillance, in accordance with his conviction that a successful ruler leaves nothing to Providence that he can discover and regulate for himself. "Trust in God, but tie your camel." By this means, as well as by personal influence and exhortation, "Disaffected" were controlled and ultimately converted into good Muslim; for the more cautious of them—those who waited to see how events would shape—soon assured themselves of Mahomet's capacity, and the weakly passive were caught in the swirl of enthusiasm surrounding the Prophet that continually drew unto itself all conditions of men within its ever-widening circle.

Having organised his own followers, and secured their immunity from internal strife, Mahomet was forced to turn his attention to the Jewish element within his adopted city, and to decide swiftly his policy towards the three Israelite tribes who comprised the wealthier and trading population of Medina.

From the first, Mahomet's desires were in the direction of a federal union, wherein each party would follow his own faith and have control of his own tribal affairs and finances, save when the necessity of mutual protection against enemies called for a union of forces. Again Mahomet framed his policy upon the doctrine of opportunism. His ultimate aim was beyond doubt to unite both Jews and Medinans under his rule in a common religious and political bond, but he recognised the present impossibility of such action in view of the Jews' greater stability and the weakness of his party within the city. His negotiations and conciliations with the Jews offer one of the many examples of his supreme skill as a statesman.

The Jews themselves, taken almost unawares by the suddenness of Mahomet's entry into their civic life, agreed to the treaty he proposed, and acquiesced unconsciously in his subtle attempts to merge the two faiths into a whole wherein Islam would be the dominant factor. When Mahomet made Jerusalem his Kibla, or direction of prayer, and emphasised the connection between Jewish and Arabian history, they suffered these advances, and agreed to a treaty which would have formed the foundations of a political and social convergence and ultimate absorption of their own nation.

Mahomet knew that federalism with the Jews was a necessary step to his desired end, and therefore he drew up a treaty wherein mutual protection against outward enemies, as well as against internal sedition, was assured. Hospitality was to be freely rendered and demanded, and neither party was to support an Infidel against a Believer. Guarantees for mutual security were exchanged, and it was agreed that each should be free to worship in his own fashion. The treaty throws light upon the clan-system still obtaining in seventh-century Arabia. The Jews were their own masters in the ordering of their lives, as were the Medinan tribes, even after many years of neighbourhood and frequent interchange of commerce and mutual assurances. The most significant political work achieved by Mahomet, the planting of the federal, and later, the national idea in Arabia in place of the tribal one, was thus inaugurated, and throughout the development of his political power it will be seen that the struggles between himself and the surrounding peoples virtually hinged upon the acceptance or rejection of it.

The Jews, with their narrow conception of the political unit, could acquiesce neither in federalism nor in union, and as soon as Mahomet perceived their incapacity he became implacable, and either drove them forth or compelled their submission by terror and slaughter. But for the present his policy and prudence dictated compromise, and he was strong enough to achieve his will.

The political and social problems of his embryo state had found temporary solution, and Mahomet was free to turn his attention to external foes. In his attitude towards those who had persecuted him he evinced more than ever his determination to build up not only a religious society, but a powerful temporal state.

The Meccans would have been content to leave matters as they stood, and were quite prepared to let Mahomet establish his power at Medina unmolested, provided they were given like immunity from attacks. But from the beginning other plans filled the Prophet's thoughts, and though revenge for his privations was declared to be the instigator of his attacks on the Kureisch trade, the determining motive must be looked for much more deeply. The great project of the harassment and final overthrow of the Kureisch was dimly foreshadowed in Mahomet's mind, and he became ever more deeply aware of the part that must be played therein by the sword.

As yet he hesitated to acclaim war as the supreme arbiter in his own and his followers' destinies, for the valour of his levies and the skill of his leaders was unproved. The forays undertaken before the battle of Bedr are really nothing more than essays by the Muslim in the game of war, and it was not until proof of their power against the Kureisch had been given that Mahomet gave up his future policy into the keeping of that bright disastrous deity that lures all sons of men. In a measure it was true that the clash between Mahomet and the Kureisch was unavoidable, but that it loomed so large upon the horizon of Medina's policy is due to the Prophet's determination to strike immediately at the wealth and security of his rival. Lust for plunder, too, added its weight to Mahomet's reprisals against Mecca; even if that city was content to leave him in peace, still the Kureischite caravans to Bostra and Syria, passing so near to Medina, were too tempting to be ignored.

Along these age-old routes Meccan merchandise still travelled its devious way, at the mercy of sun and desert storms and the unheeding fierceness of that cataclysmic country, a prey to any marauding tribes, and dependent for its existence upon the strength of its escort. And since plunder is sweeter than labour, every chief with swift riders and good spearmen hoped to gain his riches at Meccan expense. But their attempts were for the most part abortive, chiefly because of the lack of cohesion and generalship; until Mahomet none really constituted a serious menace to the Kureischite wealth.

In Muharram 622 (April) the Hegira took place, and six months sufficed Mahomet to establish his power securely enough to be able to send out his first expedition against the Kureisch in Ramadan (December) of the same year. The party was led by Hamza, whose soldier qualities were only at the beginning of their development, and probably consisted of a few Muslim horsemen on their beautiful swift mounts and one or two spearmen, and possibly several warriors skilled in the use of arrows. They sallied forth from Medina and went to meet the caravan as it prepared to pass by their town. The Kureisch had placed Abu Jahl in command—a man whose invincible hatred for Islam and the Prophet had manifested itself in the persecution at Mecca, and whose hostility increased as the Muslim power advanced.

The caravan was guarded, but none too strongly, and Hamza's troop pursued and had almost attacked it when a Bedouin chief of the desert more powerful than either party interposed and compelled the Muslim to withdraw, while he forbade Abu Jahl to pursue them or attempt revenge. So the caravan continued its way unmolested into Syria and there exchanged its gums, leather, and frankincense for the silks and precious metals, the fine stuffs and luxurious draperies which made the Syrian markets a vivid medley of sheen and gloss, stored with bright colours and burnished surfaces shimmering in the hot radiance of the East. In Jan. 623 the caravan set out homeward "on its lone journey o'er the desert," and again the Muslim sent out an attacking party in the hope of securing this larger prize. But the Kureisch were wise and had provided themselves with a stronger escort before which the Muslim could do nothing but retreat—not, however, before they had sent a few tentative arrows at the cavalcade. Obeida, their leader and a cousin of Mahomet, gave the command to shoot, and is renowned henceforth as "he who shot the first arrow for Islam."

After a month another essay was made upon a northward-bound caravan by Sa'd, again without success, for he had miscalculated dates and missed his quarry by some days. Each leader on his return to Medina was received with honour by Mahomet as one who had shown his prowess in the cause of Isalm and presented with a white banner.

So far the prophet himself had not taken the field; now, however, in the summer and autumn of 623, in spite of signs that all was not well with the Jewish alliance at home, Mahomet took the field in person and conducted three larger but still unsuccessful expeditions; the last attacking levy of October 623 consisted of 200 men, but even then Mahomet was able to effect nothing against the Kureischite escort. The attempted raid had nevertheless an important outcome, for by this exhibition of strength Mahomet succeeded in convincing a neighboring desert tribe, hitherto friendly to Mecca, of the advisability of seeking alliance with the Muslim.

The treaty between Mahomet and the Bedouin tribe marks the beginning of a significant development in his foreign polity. Like the Romans, and all military nations, he knew the worth of making advantageous alliances, while he was clear-sighted enough to realise that the struggle with Mecca was inevitable. During the months preceding the battle of Bedr he concluded several treaties with desert tribes, and it is to this policy he owes in part his power to maintain his aggressive attitude towards the Kureisch, for with the alliance of the tribes around the caravan routes Mahomet could be sure of hampering the Meccan trade.

While the Prophet was in the field he left representatives to care for the affairs of his city. These representatives were designated by him, and were always members of his personal following. Ali and Abu Bekr were most often chosen until All proved his worth as a warrior, and so usually accompanied or commanded the expeditionary force. The representatives held their authority direct from Mahomet, and had in all matters the identical power of the Prophet during his absence. It speaks well for the loyalty and acumen of these ministers that Mahomet was enabled to leave the city so often and so confidently, and that the government continued as if under his personal supervision.

Whether the Jews were overbold because of Mahomet's frequent absences, or whether they now became conscious of the trend of Mahomet's policy towards the absorption of the Jewish element within the city into Islam, will never be made clear, beyond the fact that the Jewish tribes were not enthusiastic in their union with the Muslim, and that their national character precluded them from accepting an alliance that threatened the autonomy of their religion. It is, however, certain that the discontent of the Jews voiced itself more and more loudly as the year advanced. The suras of the period are full of revilings and threats against them, and form a greater contrast coming after the later Meccan suras wherein Israel was honoured and its heroes held up as examples. A few Jews had been won over to his cause, but the mass showed themselves either hostile or indifferent to the federal idea. As yet no definite sundering of relationships had occurred, but everything pointed to a speedy dissolution of the treaty unless one side or the other moderated its views.

The autumn of 628 saw Mahomet fully established in Medina. He had made his worth known by his energy and organising power, by his devotion to Allah and his zeal for the faith he had founded. The Medinans regarded him already as their natural leader, and he had definitely adopted their city as his headquarters. Through his skill as a statesman and his loyalty to an idea he wrought out, the foundations of his future state, and if the latter months of 623 saw him not yet strong enough to overcome the Meccans, at least he was so firmly established that he could afford to dispense with any overtures to the increasingly hostile Jews, and he had gained sufficient adherents to allow him to contemplate with equanimity the prospect of a sharp and prolonged struggle with the Kureisch.

CHAPTER X

THE SECESSION OF THE JEWS

"Even though thou shouldst bring every kind of sign to those who have received the Scriptures, yet Thy Kibla they will not adopt; nor shalt thou adopt their Kibla; nor will one part of them adopt the Kibla of the other."—The Kuran.

Mahomet realised the position of affairs at Medina too acutely to allow of his undertaking in person any predatory expeditions against the Kureisch during the autumn and winter of 623. The Jews were chafing under his tacit assumption of State control, and although their murmurings had not reached the recklessness of strife, still both their leaders and the Muslim perceived that their disaffection was inevitable. Insecurity at home, however, did not prevent him from sending out an expedition in Rajab (October) of that year under Abdallah. Rajab is a sacred month in the Mohamedan calendar, one in which war is forbidden. Strictly, therefore, in sending out an expedition at all just then Mahomet was transgressing against the laws of that religion which, purged of its idolatries, he claimed as his own. But it was a favourable opportunity to attack the Kureischite caravan on its way to Taif, and therefore Mahomet recked nothing of the prohibition.

Taif was a very distant objective for an expeditionary band from Medina, and that Mahomet contemplated attack upon his enemy by a company so far removed from its base is convincing proof, should any be needed, of his confidence in his followers' prowess and his conciliation of the tribes lying between the two hostile cities.

Sealed orders were given to Abdallah, with instructions not to open the parchment until he was two days south of Medina. At sunset on the second day he came with his eight followers to a well in the midst of the desert. There under the few date palms, which gave them rough shelter, he broke the seal and read:

"When thou readest this writing depart unto Nakhla, between Taif and Mecca; there lie in wait for the Kureisch, and bring thy comrades news concerning them."

As Abdallah read his mind alternated between apprehension and daring, and turning to his companions he took counsel of them.

"Mahomet has commanded me to go to Nakhla and there await the Kureisch; also he has commanded me to say unto you whoever desireth martyrdom for Islam let him follow me, and whoever will not suffer it, let him turn back. As for me, I am resolved to carry out the commands of God's Prophet"

Then one and all the eight companions assured him they would not forsake him until the quest was achieved. At dawn they resumed their march and arrived at length at Nakhla, where they encountered the Kureisch caravan laden with spice and leather. Now, it was the last day of the month of Rajab, wherein it was unlawful to fight, wherefore the Muslim took counsel, saying:

"If we fight not this day, they will elude us and escape."

But the Prophet's implied command was strong enough to induce initiative and hardihood in the small attacking party. They bore down upon the Kureisch, showering arrows in their path, so that one man was killed and several wounded. The rest forsook their merchandise and fled, leaving behind them two prisoners, whose retreat had been cut off. Abdallah was left in possession of the field, and joyfully he returned to Medina, bearing with him the first plunder captured by the Muslim.

But his return led Mahomet into a quandary from which there seemed no escape. Politically, he was bound to approve Abdallah's deed; religiously, he could neither laud it nor share the fruits of it. For days the spoils remained undivided, but Abdallah was not punished or even reprimanded.

Meanwhile, the Jews and the Kureisch vied with one another in execrating Mahomet, and even his own people murmured against him. It was clearly time that an authoritative sanction should be given to the deed, and accordingly in the sura, "The Cow," we have the revelation from Allah proclaiming the greater culpability of the Infidels and of those who would stir up civil strife:

"They will ask thee concerning war in the Sacred Month. Say: To war therein is bad, but to turn aside from the cause of God, and to have no faith in Him, and in the Sacred Temple, and to drive out its people, is worse in the sight of God; civil strife is worse than bloodshed."

No possible doubt must be cast in this and similar cases upon Mahomet's sincerity. The Kuran was the vehicle of the Lord; he had used it to proclaim his unity and power and his warnings to the unrighteous. Now that Islam had recognised his august and indissoluble majesty, and had accorded the throne of Heaven and the governance of earth to him indivisibly, the world was split up into Believers and Unbelievers. The Kuran, therefore, must of necessity cease to be merely the proclamation of divine unity that it had been and become the vehicle for definite orders and regulations, the outcome of those theocratic ideas upon which Mahomet's creed was founded. The justification would not appeal to the people unless Allah's sanction supported it, and Mahomet realised with all his ardour of faith that the transgression was slight compared with the result achieved towards the progress of Islam. The Prophet therefore received, with Allah's approval, a fifth of the spoil, but the captives he released after receiving ransom.

"This," says the historian, "was the first booty that Mahomet obtained, the first captives they seized, and the first life they took." The significance of the event was vividly felt throughout Islam, and Abdallah, its hero, received at Mahomet's hands the title of "Amir-al-Momirim," Commander of the Faithful—a title which recalls inseparably the cruelty and magnificence, the glamour and rapacity, of Arabian Bagdad under Haroun-al-Raschid. The valorous enterprise had now been achieved, the Kureisch caravan was despoiled, and the Kureisch themselves wrought into fury against the Prophet's insolence; but more than all, the channel of Mahomet's policy of warfare became thereby so deeply carved that he could not have effaced it had he desired. Henceforth his creative genius limited itself to the deepening of its course and the direction of its outlet.

The Jews had not rested content with murmuring against Mahomet's rule, they sought to embarrass him by active sedition. One of their first attempts against Mahomet's regime was to stir up strife between the Refugees and Helpers. In this they would have been successful but for Mahomet's efficient system of espionage, a method upon which he relied throughout his life. Failing to foment a rebellion in secret they proceeded to open hostilities, and the Muslim, jealous for their faith, retaliated by contempt and estrangement. During the winter of 623 personal attack was made by the mob upon Mahomet. The people were hounded on by their leaders to stone the Prophet, but he was warned in time and escaped their assaults.

The popular fury was merely the reflex of a fundamental division of thought between the opposing parties. The Jewish and Muslim systems could never coalesce, for each claimed the dominance and ignored all compromise. The age-long, hallowed traditions of the Jews which supported a theocracy as unyielding as any conception of Divine sovereignty preached by Mahomet, found themselves faced with a new creative force rapidly evolving its own legends, and strong enough in its enthusiasm to overwhelm their own. The Rabbis felt that Mahomet and his warrior heroes—Ali, Omar, Othman, and the rest—would in time dislodge from their high places their own peculiar saints, just as they saw Mahomet with Abu Bekr and his personnel of administrators and informers already overriding their own councillors in the civil and military departments of their state. The old regime could not amalgamate with the new, for that would mean absorption by its more vigorous neighbour, and the Jewish spirit is exclusive in essence and separatist perforce. Mahomet took no pains to conciliate his allies; they had made a treaty with him in the days of his insecurity and he was grateful, but now his position in Medina was beyond assailment, and he was indifferent to their goodwill. As their aggression increased he deliberately withdrew his participation in their religious life, and severed his connection with their rites and ordinances.

The Kibla of the Muslim, whither at every prayer they turned their faces, and which he had declared to be the Temple at Jerusalem, scene of his embarkation upon the wondrous "Midnight Journey," was now changed to the Kaaba at Mecca. What prevision or prophetic inspiration prompted Mahomet to turn his followers' eyes away from the north and fix them upon their former home with its fierce and ruthless heat, the materialisation, it seemed, of his own inexorable and passionate aims? Henceforth Mecca became unconsciously the goal of every Muslim, the desired city, to be fought for and died for, the dwelling-place of their Prophet, the crown of their faith.

The Jewish Fast of Atonement, which plays so important a part in Semite faith and doctrine, had been made part of the Muslim ritual in 622, while a federal union still seemed possible, but the next year such an amalgamation could not take place. In Ramadan (Dec. to January), therefore, Mahomet instituted a separate fast for the Faithful. It was to extend throughout the Sacred Month in which the Kuran had first been sent down to men. Its sanctity became henceforth a potent reminder for the Muslim of his special duties towards Allah, of the reverence meet to be accorded to the Divine Upholder of Islam. During all the days of Ramadan, no food or drink might pass a Muslim lip, nor might he touch a woman, but the moment the sun's rim dipped below the horizon he was absolved from the fast until dawn. No institution in Islam is so peculiarly sacred as Ramadan, and none so scrupulously observed, even when, by the revolution of the lunar year, the fast falls during the bitter heat of summer. It is a characteristic ordinance, and one which emphasises the vivid Muslim apprehension of the part played by abstention in their religious code. At the end of the fast—that is, upon the sight of the next new moon—Mahomet proclaimed a festival, Eed-al-Fitr, which was to take the place of the great Jewish ceremony of rejoicing.

At this time, too, Mahomet, evidently bent on consolidating his religious observances and regulating their conduct, decreed a fresh institution, with parallels in no religion—the Adzan, or call to prayer. Mahomet wished to summon the Believers to the Mosque, and there was no way except to ring a bell such as the Christians use, which rite was displeasing to the Faithful. Indeed, Mahomet is reported later to have said, "The bell is the devil's musical instrument."

But Abdallah, a man of profound faith and love for Islam, received thereafter a vision wherein a "spirit, in the guise of man, clad in green garments," appeared to him and summoned him to call the Believers to prayer from the Mosque at every time set apart for devotion.

"Call ye four times 'God is great,' and then, 'I bear witness that there is no God but God, and Mahomet is His Prophet. Come unto prayer, come unto salvation. God is great; there is no God but Him.'"

"A true vision," declared Mahomet. "Go and teach it to Bilal, that he may call to prayer, for he has a better voice than thou."

When Bilal, a slave, received the command, he went up to the Mosque, and climbing its highest minaret, he cried aloud his summons, adding at each dawn:

"Prayer is better than sleep, prayer is better than sleep."

And when Omar heard the call, he went to Mahomet and declared that he had the previous night received the same vision.

And Mahomet answered him, "Praise be to Allah!"

Therewith was inaugurated the most characteristic observance in Islam, the one which impresses itself very strongly upon the Western traveller as he hears in the dimness of every dawning, before the sun's edge is seen in the east, the voices of the Muezzin from each mosque in the city proclaiming their changeless message, their insistent command to prayer and praise. He sees the city leap into magical life, the dark figures of the Muslim hurrying to the Holy Place that lies shimmering in the golden light of early day, and knows that, behind this outward manifestation, lies a faith, at root incomprehensible by reason of its aloofness from the advancing streams of modern thought, a faith spiritually impotent, since it flees from mysticism, generating an energy which has expended its vital force in conquest, only to find itself too intellectually backward and physically sluggish to gather in prosperity the fruits of its attainments. Its lack of imagination, its utter ignorance of the lure of what is strange, have been responsible for its achievement of stupendous tasks, for the driving energy behind was never appalled by anticipation, nor checked by any realisation of coming stress and terror. And the same qualities that led the Muslim to world-conquest thereafter caused their downfall, for their minds could not visualise that world of imagination necessary for any creative science, while they were not attuned in intellect for the reception of such generative ideas as have contributed to the philosophic and speculative development of the Western world.

All the characteristics which distinguish Islam to the making and the blasting of its fortunes may be found in embryo in the small Medinan community; for their leader, by his own creative ardour, imposed upon his flock every idea which shaped the form and content of its future career from its rising even to its zenith and decline.

CHAPTER XI

THE BATTLE OF BEDR

"They plotted, but God plotted, and of plotters is God the best."—The Koran.

Mahomet's star, now continually upon the ascendant, flamed into sudden glory in Ramadan of the second year of the Hegira. Its brilliance and the bewilderment caused by its triumphant continuance is reflected in all the chronicles and legends clustered around that period.

If Nakhlu had been an achievement worthy of God's emissary, the victory which followed it was an irrefutable argument in favour of Mahomet's divinely ordained rulership of the Arabian peoples. It appeared to the Muslim, and even to contemporary hostile tribes, nothing less than a stupendous proof of their championship by God. Muslim poets and historians are never weary of expatiating upon the glories achieved by their tiny community with little but abiding zeal and supreme faith with which to confound their foes. No military event in the life of the Prophet called forth such rejoicings from his own lips as the triumph at Bedr:

"O ye Meccans, if ye desired a decision, now hath the decision come to you. It will be better for you if ye give over the struggle. If ye return to it, we will return, and your forces, though they be many, shall never avail you aught, for God is with the Faithful."

Through the whole of Sura viii the strain of exultation runs, the presentment in dull words of fierce and splendid courage wrought out into victory in the midst of the storms and lightnings of Heaven.

Such an earth-shaking event, the effects of which reached far beyond its immediate environment, received fitting treatment at the hands of all Arabian chronicles, so that we are enabled to reconstruct the events preceding the battle itself, its action and result, with a vivid completeness that is often denied us in the lesser events.

The caravan under Abu Sofian, about thirty or forty strong, which had eluded Mahomet and reached Syria, was now due to return to Mecca with its bartered merchandise. Mahomet was determined that this time it should not escape, and that he would exact from it full penalty of the vengeance he owed the Meccans for his insults and final expulsion from their city. As soon as the time for its approach drew nigh, Mahomet sent two scouts to Hama, north of Medina, who were to bring tidings to him the moment they caught sight of its advancing dust. But Abu Sofian had been warned of Mahomet's activity and turned off swiftly to the coast, keeping the seaward route, while he sent a messenger to Mecca with the news that an attack by the Muslim was meditated.

Dhamdham, sent by his anxious leader, arrived in the city after three days' journey in desperate haste across the desert, and flung himself from his camel before the Kaaba. There he beat the camel to its knees, cut off its ears and nose, and put the saddle hind foremost. Then, rending his garments, he cried with a loud voice:

"Help, O Kureisch, your caravan is pursued by Mahomet!"

With one accord the Meccan warriors, angered by the news that spread wildly among the populace, assembled before their holy place and swore a great oath that they would uphold their dignity and avenge their loss upon the upstart followers of a demented leader. Every man who could bear arms prepared in haste for the expedition, and those who could not fight found young men as their representatives. In the midst of all the tumult and eager resolutions to exterminate the Muslim, so runs the tale, there were few who would listen to Atikah, the daughter of Abd-al-Muttalib.

"I have dreamed three nights ago, that the Kureisch will be called to arms in three days and will perish. Behold the fulfilment of my dream! Woe to the Kureisch, for their slaughter is foretold!"

But she was treated as of no account, a woman and frail, and the army set out upon its expedition in all the bravery of that pomp-loving nation.

With Abu Jahl at its head, and accompanied by slave girls with lutes and tabrets, who were to gladden the eyes and minister to the pleasure of its warriors, the Kureisch army moved on through the desert towards its destined goal; but we are told by a recorder, "dreams of disaster accompanied it, nor was its sleep tranquil for the evil portents that appeared therein." Thus, apprehensive but dauntless, the Meccan army advanced to Safra, one day's march from Bedr, where it encountered messengers from Abu Sofian, who announced that the caravan had eluded the Muslim and was safe.

Then arose a debate among the Kureisch as to their next course. Many desired to return to Mecca, deeming their purpose accomplished now that the caravan was secure from attack, but the bolder amongst them were anxious to advance, and the more deliberative favoured this also, because by so doing they might hope to overawe Mahomet into quietude. But before all there was the safety of their homes to consider, and they were fearful lest an attack by a hostile tribe, the Beni Bekr, might be made upon Mecca in the absence of its fighting men. Upon receiving assurances of good faith from a tribe friendly to both, they dismissed that fear and resolved to advance, so that they might compel Mahomet to abandon his attacks upon their merchandise.

This proceeding seemed a reasonable and politic measure, until it was viewed in the light of its consequences, and indeed, judging from ordinary calculation, such a host could have no other effect than a complete rout upon such a small and inefficient band as Mahomet's followers. Therefore, in estimating, if they did at all carefully, the forces matched against them, the Kureisch found themselves materially invincible, though they had not reckoned the spiritual factor of enthusiasm which transcended their own physical superiority.

These events had taken over nine days, and meanwhile Mahomet had not been idle. His two spies had brought news of the approach of the caravan, but beyond that meagre information he knew nothing. The Kureischite activity thereafter was swallowed up in the vastnesses of the desert, which drew a curtain as effective as death around the opposing armies.

But news of the caravan's advance was sufficient for the Prophet. With the greatest possible speed he collected his army—not, we are told, without some opposition from the fearful among the Medinan population, who were anxious to avoid any act which might bring down upon them the ruthless Meccan hosts. Legend has counted as her own this gathering together of the Muslim before Bedr, and translating the engendered enthusiasm into imaginative fact, has woven a pattern of barbaric colours, wherein deeds are transformed by the spirit which prompts them. The heroes panted for martyrdom, and each craved to be among the first to pour forth his blood in the sacred cause. They crowded to battle on camels and on foot. Abu Bekr in his zeal walked every step of the way, which he regarded as the road to supreme benediction. Mahomet himself led his valorous band, mounted on a camel with Ali by his side, having before him two black flags borne by standard-bearers whose strength and bravery were the envy of the rest. He possessed only seventy camels and two horses, and the riders were chosen by lot. Behind marched or rode the flower of Islam's warriors and statesmen—Abu Bekr, Omar, Hamza, and Zeid, whose names already resounded through Islam for valiant deeds; Abdallah, with Mahomet's chosen leaders of expeditions; the rank and file, three hundred strong, regardless of what perils might overtake them, intent on plunder and the upholding of their vigorous faith, sallied forth from Medina as soon as they could be equipped, and took the direct road to Mecca. On reaching Safra, for reasons we are not told, they turned west to Bedr, a halting-place on the Syrian road, possibly hoping to catch the caravan on its journey westwards towards the sea.

But Abu Sofian was too quick for them. Mahomet's scouts had only reached Bedr, reconnoitered and retired, when Abu Sofian approached the well within its precincts and demanded of a man belonging to a neighbouring tribe if there were strangers in the vicinity.

"I have seen none but two men, O Chief," he replied; "they came to the well to water their camels."

But he had been bribed by Mahomet, and knew well they were Muslim.

Abu Sofian was silent, and looked around him carefully. Suddenly he started up as he caught sight of their camels' litter, wherein were visible the small date stones peculiar to Medinan palms.

"Camels from Yathreb!" he cried quickly; "these be the scouts of Mahomet." Then he gathered his company together and departed hastily towards the sea. He despatched a messenger to Mecca to tell of the caravan's safety, and a little later heard with joy of his countrymen's progress to oppose Mahomet.

"Doth Mahomet indeed imagine that it will be this time as in the affair of the Hadramate (slain at Nakhla)? Never! He shall know that it is otherwise!"

But the army that caused such joy to Abu Sofian created nothing but apprehension in Mahomet's camp. He knew the caravan had eluded him, and now there was a greater force more than three times his own advancing on him. Hurriedly he convened a council of war, whereat his whole following urged an immediate advance. The excitement had now fully captured their tumultuous souls, and there was more danger for Mahomet in a retreat than in an attack. An immediate advance was therefore decided upon, and Mahomet sent Ali, on the day before the battle, to reconnoitre, as they were nearing Bedr. The same journey which told Abu Sofian of the presence of the Muslim also resulted for them in the capture of three water-carriers by Ali, who dragged them before Mahomet, where they were compelled to give the information he wanted, and from them he learned the disposition and strength of the enemy.

The valley of Bedr is a plain, with hills flanking it to the north and east. On the west are small sandy hillocks which render progress difficult, especially if the ground is at all damp from recent rains. Through this shallow valley runs the little stream, having at its south-western extremity the springs and wells which give the place its importance as a halting stage. Command of the wells was of the highest importance, but as yet neither army had obtained it, for the Muslim had not taken up their final position, and the Kureisch were hemmed in by the sandy ground in front of them.

The wretched water-carriers being brought before Mahomet at first declared they knew nothing, but after some time confessed they were Abu Jahl's servants.

"And where is the abiding place of Abu Jahl?"

"Beyond the sand-hills to the east."

"And how many of his countrymen abide with him?"

"They are numerous; I cannot tell; they are as numerous as leaves."

"On one day nine, the next ten."

"Then they number 950 men," exclaimed the Prophet to Ali; "take the men away."

Mahomet now called a council of generals, and it was decided to advance up the valley to the farther side of the wells, so as to secure the water-supply, and destroy all except the one they themselves needed. This manoeuvre was carried out successfully, and the Muslim army encamped opposite the Kureisch, at the foot of the western hills and separated from their adversaries by the low sandy hillocks in front of them. A rough hut of palm branches was built for Mahomet whence he could direct the battle, and where he could retire for counsel with Abu Bekr, and for prayer.

Both sides had now made their dispositions, and there remained nothing but to wait till daybreak. That night the rain descended upon the doomed Kureisch like the spears of the Lord, whelming their sandy soil and churning up the rising ground in front of the troops into a quagmire of bottomless mud. The clouds were tempered towards the higher Muslim position, and the water drained off the hilly land.

"See, the Lord is with us; he has sent his heavy rain upon our enemies," declared Mahomet, looking from his hut in the early dawn, weary with anxiety for the issue of this fateful hour, but strong in faith and confident in the favour of Allah. Then he retired to the hut for prayer and contemplation.

"O Allah, forget not thy promise! O Lord, if this little band be vanquished idolatry will prevail and thy pure worship cease from off the earth."

He set himself to the encouragement and instruction of his troops. He had no cavalry with which to cover an advance, and he therefore ordered his troops to remain firm and await the oncoming rush until the word to charge was given.

But on no account were they to lose command of the wells. Drawn up in several lines, their champions in front and Mahomet with Abu Bekr to direct them from the rear, the little troop of Muslim awaited the onslaught of their greater foes.

But dissent had broken out among the Kureisch generals. Obi, one of their best warriors, perhaps feeling the confident carelessness of the Kureisch was misplaced, wanted to go back without attacking. He was overruled after much discussion and some bad feeling by Abu Jahl, who declared that if they refrained from attack now all the land would ring with their cowardice. So a general advance was ordered, and the Kureisch champions led the way.

The battle began, as most battles of primitive times, by a series of single combats, one champion challenging another to fight. The glory of being the first Muslim to kill a Meccan in this encounter fell to Hamza. Aswad of the Kureisch swore to drink of the water of those wells guarded by the Muslim. Hamza opposed, and his first sword stroke severed the leg of Aswad; but he, undaunted, crawled on until at the fountain he was slain by Hamza before its waters passed his lips. Now three champions of the Kureisch came forward to challenge three Muslim of equal birth. Hamza, Ali, and Obeida answered the charge, and in front of the opposing ranks three Homeric conflicts raged.

Hamza, the lion of God, and Ali, the sword of the faith, quickly overcame their opponents, but Obeida was wounded before he could spear his man. The sight gave courage to the Kureisch, and now the main body of them pressed on, seeking to overwhelm the Muslim by sheer weight. The heavy ground impeded their movements, and they came on slowly with what anxious expectation on the part of Mahomet's soldiers, whom their Prophet had commanded to await his signal.

When the Kureisch were near enough Mahomet lifted his hand:

"Ya Mansur amit!" (Ye conquerors, strike!) he cried, pointing with outstretched finger at the close ranks bearing down upon them; "Paradise awaits him who lays down his life for Islam."

The Muslim with a wild cry dashed forward against their foe. But the Kureisch were brave and they were numerous, and the Muslim were few and almost untutored. The battle raged, surging like foam within the narrow valley; its waves now roaring almost up to the Prophet's vantage ground, now retreating in eddies towards the rear of the Kureisch, under a lowering sky, whose wind-swept clouds seemed to reflect the strife in the Heavens.

"Behold Gabriel with a thousand angels charging down upon the Infidels!" cried Mahomet, as a blast of wind tore shrieking down the valley. "See Muhail and Seraphil with their troops rush to the help of God's chosen."

Then as the Muslim seemed to waver, pressed back by the mass of their enemies, he appeared in their midst, and, taking a handful of dust, cast it in the face of the foe:

"Let their faces be confounded!"

The Muslim, caught by the magnetism of Mahomet's presence, seized by the immortal energy which radiated from him, rallied their strength. With a shout they bore down upon the Kureisch, who wavered and broke beneath this inspired onrush, within whose vigour dwelt all Mahomet's surcharged ambition and indomitable aims. He commanded the attack to be followed up at once, and the Kureisch, hampered in their retreat by the marshy ground, fell in confusion, their ranks shattered, their champions crushed in the welter of spears and horsemen, swords, armour, sand, blood, and the bodies of men.

The order went forth from Mahomet to spare as much as possible his own house of Hashim, but otherwise the slaughter was as remorseless as the temper of the Muslim ensured. Of the Prophet's army, so tell the Chronicles, only fourteen were killed, but of the Kureisch the dead numbered forty-nine, with a like haul of prisoners. Abu Jahl was among those sorely wounded; but when Abdallah saw him lying helpless, he recognised him, and slew him without a word. Then having cut off his head, he brought the prize to Mahomet.

"It is the head of God's enemy," cried the Prophet as he gazed on it in exaltation; "it is more acceptable to me than the choicest camel in all Arabia."

The broken remnants of the Kureisch army journeyed slowly back to Mecca through the same desert that had seen all the bravery and splendour of their advance, and the news of their terrible fate preceded them. All the city was draped in cloths of mourning, for there was no distinguished house that did not bewail its dead. One alone did not weep—Hind, wife of Abu Sofian, went forth to meet her husband.

"What doest thou with unrent garments? Knowest thou not the affliction that hath fallen on this thy city?"

"I will not weep," replied Hind, "until this wrong has been avenged. When thou hast gone forth, hast conquered this accursed, then will I mourn for those who are slain this day. Nay, my lord, I will not deck myself, nor perfume my hair, nor come near thy couch until I see the avenging of this humiliation."

Then Abu Sofian swore a great oath that he would immediately collect men and take the field once more against Islam.

There remained now for the victors but the distribution of the spoil and the decision of the fate of the prisoners. The less valuable of these were put to death, their bodies cast into a pit, but the

Muslim took the rest with them, hoping for ransom. The spoil was taken up in haste, and the Prophet repaired joyfully to Safra, where he proposed to divide it. But there contention arose, as was almost inevitable, over the distribution of the wealth, and so acute did the disaffection become that Mahomet revealed the will of Allah concerning it:

"And know ye, when ye have taken any booty, a fifth part belongeth to God and to the Apostle, and to the near of kin and to orphans and to the poor, and to the wayfarer, if ye believe in God, and in that which we have sent down to our servant on the day of the victory, the day of the meeting of the Hosts." As part of his due, Mahomet took the famous sword Dhul Ficar, which has gathered around it as many legends as the weapons of classical heroes, and which hereafter never left him whenever he took command of his followers in battle. So the Muslim, flushed with victory, laden with spoil, returned to Medina, whose entire population assembled to accord them triumphal entry.

"Abu Jahl, the sinner, is slain," cried the little children, catching the phrase from their parents' lips.

"Abu Jahl, the sinner, is slain, and the foes of Islam laid low!" was cried from the mosque and market-place, from minaret and house-top. "Allah Akbar Islam!"

The great testing day had come and was past. In open fight, before a host of their foes, the Muslim with smaller numbers had prevailed. The effect upon Medina and upon Mahomet's later career cannot be overestimated. It was indeed a turning point, whence Mahomet proceeded irrevocably upon the road to success and fame. Reverses hereafter he certainly had, and at times the outlook was almost insuperably dark, but no misfortune or gloom could dull the splendour of that day at Bedr, when besides his own slender following, the hosts of the Lord, whose turbans glowed like crowns, led by Gabriel in golden armour, had fought for him and vanquished his foes. The glory of this battle was the lamp by which he planned his future wins.

At Medina the Disaffected were triumphantly gathered beneath his banner; his position became, for the time at least, established. No longer did he need to conciliate, flatter, spy upon the various factions within his walls. His prisoners were kindly treated, and some converted by these means to the faith he had vainly sought to impose upon them. Affairs within the city were organised and consolidated. Registers were prepared, the famous "Registers of Omar," which were to contain the names of all those who had given distinguished service to the cause of Allah, and to confer upon them exalted rank. The three hundred names inscribed therein were the embryo of a Muslim aristocracy, constituting, in fact, a peerage of Islam. Mahomet's religious ordinances were strengthened and confirmed, while his faith received that homage paid to success which had raised its founder from the commander of a small band of religionists to the chief of a prosperous city, the leader of an efficient army, the head of a community which held within itself the future dominion of Arabia, of western Asia, southern Europe, in fact, the greater part of the middle world.

More than ever Mahomet perceived that his success lay in the sword. Bedr set the seal upon his acceptance of warfare as a means of propaganda. Henceforth the sword becomes to him the bright but awful instrument through which the will of Allah is achieved. In the measure that he trusted its power and confided to it his own destiny and that of his followers, so did war exact of him its ceaseless penalty, urging him on continually, through motives of policy and self-defence, until he became its slave, compelled to continue along the path appointed him, or perish by that very instrument by which his power had been wrought. Henceforward his activities consist chiefly of wars aggressive and defensive, while the religion actuating them receives slighter notice, because the main thesis has been established in his own state and requires the force of arms to obtain its supremacy over alien races.

After Bedr, the poet and Prophet becomes the administrator and Prophet. The quietude and meditation of the Meccan hill-slopes are exchanged for the council-chamber and the battlefield, and appear upon the background of his anxious life with the glamour and aloofness of a dream-country; the inevitable turmoil and preoccupation which accompanies the direction of affairs took hold upon his life. The fervour of his nature, its remorseless activity, compelled him to legislate for his followers with that minute attention to detail almost inconceivable to the modern mind with its conceptions of the various "departments" of state.

We see him mainly through tradition, but also to a great extent in the Kuran directing the humblest details in the lives of the Muslim, organising their ritual, regulating their commerce, their usury laws, their personal cleanliness, their dietary, their social and moral relations. Regarding the multifarious duties and cares of his growing state, its almost complete helplessness in its hands, for he alone was its guiding force, it is the clearest testimony to his vital energy, his strength and sanity of brain, that he was not overwhelmed by them, and that the creative side of his nature was not crushed beyond recovery; although confronted by the clamorous demands of government and warfare, these could not touch his spiritual enthusiasm nor his glowing and changeless devotion to Allah and his cause. At the end of his long years of rule he could still say with perfect truth, "My chief delight is in prayer."

CHAPTER XII

THE JEWS AT MEDINA

"And if the people of the Book had believed, it had surely been better for them: Believers there are among them, but most of them are perverse." —*The Kuran*.

The songs of triumph over Bedr had scarcely left the lips of Muslim poets when the voice of faction was heard again in Medina. The Jews, that "stiff-necked nation," unimpressed by Mahomet's triumph, careful only of its probable effect on their own position, which effect they could not but regard as disastrous, seeing that it augured their own submission to a superior power, murmured against his success, and tried their utmost to sow dissension by the publication of contemptuous songs through the mouths of their poets and prophetesses. Not only did the Jews murmur in secret against him, but they tried hard to induce members of the original Medinan tribes to join with them in a desperate effort to throw off the Muslim yoke.

Chief among these defamers of Mahomet's prestige was Asma, a prophetess of the tribe of Beni Aus. She published abroad several libellous songs upon Mahomet, but was quickly silenced by Omeir, a blind man devoted to his leader, who felt his way to her dwelling-place at dead of night, and, creeping past her servant, slew her in the midst of her children. News of the outrage was brought to Mahomet; it was expected he would punish Omeir, but:

"Thou shalt not call him blind, but the seeing," replied the Prophet; "for indeed he hath done me great service."

The result of this ruthlessness was the official conversion of the tribe, for resistance was useless, and they had not, like the Jews, the flame of faith to keep their resistance alive. "The only alternative to a hopeless blood feud was the adoption of Islam." But the Jews, with stubborn consciousness of their own essential autonomy, preferred the more terrible alternative, and so the defamatory songs continued. When it is remembered that these compositions took the place of newspapers, were as universal and wielded as such influence, it is not to be expected that Mahomet could ignore the campaign against him. Abu Afak, a belated representative of the prophetic spirits of old, fired by the ancient glory of Israel and its present threatened degradation at the hands of this upstart, continued, in spite of all warnings, to publish abroad his contempt and hatred for the Prophet.

It was no time for half-measures. With such a ferment as this universal abuse was creating, the whole of his hard-won power might crumble. Victor though he was, it wanted only the torch of some malcontents to set alight the flame of rebellion. Therefore Mahomet, with his inexorable determination and force of will, took the only course possible in such a time. The singer was slain by his express command.

"Who will rid me of this pestilence?" he cried, and like all strong natures he had not long to wait before his will became the inspired act of another.

So fear entered into the souls of the people at Medina, and for a time there were no more disloyal songs, nor did the populace dare to oppose one who had given so efficient proof of his power.

But it was not enough for Mahomet to have silenced disaffection. He aimed at nothing less than the complete union of all Medina under his leadership and in one religious belief. To this end he went in Shawwal of the second year of the Hegira (Jan. 624) unto the Jewish tribe, the Beni Kainukaa, goldsmiths of Medina, whose works lay outside the city's confines. There he summoned their chief men in the bazaar, and exhorted them fervently to become converted to Islam. But the Kainukaa were firm in their faith and refused him with contemptuous coldness.

"O Mahomet, thou thinkest we are men akin to thine own race! Hitherto thou hast met only men unskilled in battle, and therefore couldst thou slay them. But when thou meetest us, by the God of Israel, thou shalt know we are men!" Therewith Mahomet was forced to acknowledge defeat, and he journeyed back to the city, vowing that if Allah were pleased to give him opportunity he would avenge this slight upon Islam and his own divinely appointed mission. Friction between him and the Kainukaa naturally increased, and it was therefore not long before a pretext arose. The story of a Jew's insult to a Muslim girl and its avenging by one of her co-religionists is probably only a fiction to explain Mahomet's aggression against this tribe. It is uncertain how the first definite breach arose, but it is easy to see that whatever the actual *casus belli,* such a development was inevitable.

The anger of the Prophet was aroused, for were they not presuming to oppose his will and that of Allah, whose instrument he was? He marshalled his army and put a great white banner at their head, gave the leadership to Hamza, and so marched forth to attack the rebellious Kainukaa. For fifteen days the tribe was besieged in its strongholds, until at last, beaten and discouraged, faced by scarcity of supplies, and the certainty of disease, it surrendered at discretion.

Then was shown in all its fullness the implacable despotism conceived by Mahomet as the only possible method of government, which indeed for those times and with that nation it certainly was. The order went forth for the slaying and despoiling of the Kainukaa, and the grim work began by the seizure of their armour, precious stones, gold, and goldsmith's tools. But Abdallah, chief of the Khazraj, and formerly leader of the Disaffected, became suppliant for their release. He sought audience of Mahomet, and there petitioned with many tears for the lives of his friends and kinsmen. But Mahomet turned his back upon him. Abdallah, in an ecstacy of importunity, grasped the skirt of Mahomet's garment.

"Loose thou thy hand!" cried Mahomet, while his face grew dark with anger.

But Abdallah in the boldness of desperation replied, "I will not let thee go until thou hast shown favour to my kinsmen."

Then said Mahomet, "As thou wilt not be silent, I give thee the lives of those I have taken prisoner."

Nevertheless, the exile of the tribe was enforced, and Mahomet compelled their immediate removal from the outskirts of Medina. The Prophet's later policy towards the Jews was hereby inaugurated. He set himself deliberately to break up their strongholds one by one, and did not swerve from his purpose until the whole of the hated race had been removed either by slaughter or by enforced exile from the precincts of his adopted city. He would suffer no one but himself to govern, and uprooted, with his unwavering purpose, all who refused to accept him as lord.

For about a month affairs took their normal and uninterrupted course in Medina, but in the following month, Dzul Higg (March), the last of that eventful second year, a slight disturbance of his steady work of government threatened his followers.

Abu Sofian's vow pressed sorely upon his conscience until, unable to endure inaction further, he gathered together 200 horsemen and took the highway towards Medina. He travelled by the inland road, and arrived at length at the settlements of the Beni Nadhir, one of the Jewish tribes in the vicinity of Medina. He harried their palm-gardens, burnt their cornfields, and killed two of their men. Mahomet had plundered the Meccan wealth, his allies should in turn be harassed by his victims. It was purely a private enterprise undertaken out of bravado and in fulfilment of a vow. As soon as the predatory attack had been made, Abu Sofian deemed himself absolved and prepared to return.

But Mahomet was on his traces. For five days he pursued the flying Kureisch, whose retreat turned into such a headlong rout that they threw away their sacks of meal so as to travel more lightly. Therefore the incident has been known ever since, according to the vivid Arab method of description, as the Battle of the Meal-bags. But the foe was not worthy of his pursuit, and Mahomet made no further attempt to come up with Abu Sofian, but returned at once to Medina. The attack had ended more or less in fiasco, and as a trial of strength upon either side it was negligible.

The sacred month, Dzul Higg, and the only one in which it was lawful to make the Greater Pilgrimage in far-off Mecca, was now fully upon him, and Mahomet felt drawn irresistibly to the ceremonies surrounding the ancient and now to him distorted faith. He felt compelled to acknowledge his kinship with the ancient ritual of Arabia, and to this end appointed a festival, Eed-al-Zoha, to be celebrated in this month, which was not only to take the place of the Jewish sacrificial ceremony, but to strengthen his connection with the rites still performed at Mecca, of which the Kaaba and the Black Stone formed the emblem and the goal.

In commemoration of the ceremonial slaying of victims in the vale of Mina at the end of the Greater Pilgrimage, Mahomet ordered two kids to be sacrificed at every festival, so that his people were continually reminded that at Mecca, beneath the infidel yoke, the sacred ritual, so peculiarly their own by virtue of the Abrahamic descent and their inexorable monotheism, was being unworthily performed.

The institution is important, as indicating the development of Mahomet's religious and ritualistic conceptions. In the first days of his enthusiasm he was content to enjoin worship of one God by prayer and praise, taking secondary account of forms and ceremonies. Then came the uprooting of his outward religious life and the demands of his embryo state for the manifestations essential to a communistic faith. He found Israelite beliefs uncontaminated by the worship of many Gods, and turned to their ritual in the hope of establishing with their aid a ceremonial which should incorporate their system with his own fervent faith. Now, finding no middle road between separatism and absorption possible with such a people as the Jews, and unconsciously divining that in no great length of time Islam would be sufficient unto itself, he turned again to the practices of his native religion and ancestral ceremonies. Henceforth he puts forward definitely his conception of Islam as a purified and divinely regulated form of the worship followed by his Arabian forbears, purged of its idol-worship and freed from numerous age-long corruptions.

Not only in ritual did his mind turn towards Mecca. It looms before his eyes still as the Chosen City, the city of his dreams, whose conquest and rendering back purified to the guidance of Allah he sets before his mind as the ultimate, dim-descried goal of all his intermediary wars. The Kibla had long since been changed to Mecca; thither at prayer every Muslim turned his face and directed his thoughts, and now every possible detail of ancient Meccan ritual was performed in scrupulous deference to the one God, so that when the time came and in fulfilment of his desires he set foot on its soil, no part of the ceremonies, with the lingering enthusiasm of his youth still sweet upon them, might be omitted or be allowed to lose its savour through disuse.

The third year of the Hegira began favourably for Mahomet. During the first month, Muharram, there were three small expeditions against unruly desert tribes. The Beni Ghatafan on the eastern Babylonian route were friendly to the Kureisch. This was undesirable, because they might allow the Meccan caravan to pass through in safety, and the Prophet had resolved that it should be despoiled by whichever route it journeyed, coast road or arid tableland. When therefore he received news that they were assembling in force at Carcarat-al-Kadr, a desert oasis on the confines of their territory, he marched thither in haste, hoping to catch and overcome them before they dispersed.

But the Beni Ghatafan were too wise to suffer this, and when Mahomet came to the place he found it deserted, save for some camels, left behind in the flight, which he captured and brought to Medina, deeming it useless to attempt the pursuit of his quarry through the trackless desert.

The raid in Jumad II (September) by Zeid was far more successful. Since the victory at Bedr the coast route had been entirely barred for the Kureischite caravans, and they were forced to try the central desert, which road lay through the middle tableland leading on to Babylonia and the Syrian wastes. The Meccan caravan had only reached Carada when it was met by a Muslim force under Zeid, sent by the prescience and predatory instincts of Mahomet. The guard was not strong, possibly because the Meccans thought there was little fear of attack by this route, and so Zeid was easily able to overcome his foe and secure the spoil, which amounted to many bales of goods, camels, trappings, and armour. The conquerer returned elated to Medina, where he cast the spoil at the feet of the Prophet. The usual division was made, and the whole city rejoiced over the wealth it had secured and the increasing discomfiture of its enemies.

Meanwhile matters were becoming urgent between the Muslim and the Jews. Neither the murder of their singers, nor the expulsion of the Kainukaa could silence the voice of Jewish discontent, which found its most effective mouthpiece in the poet Ka'b al' Ashraf, son of a Jewess of the tribe of the Beni Nadhir. This man had been righteously indignant at the slaughter of the Kureischite champions at Bedr. The story seemed to him so monstrous that he could not believe it.

"Is this true?" he asked the messenger; "has Mahomet verily slain these men? By the Lord, if he has done this, then is the innermost part of the earth better than the surface thereof!"

He journeyed in haste to Mecca, and when he heard the dreadful news confirmed he did his utmost to stir up the Kureisch against the murderer. As soon as he returned he published verses lamenting the disgraceful victory purchased at such a price; moreover, he also addressed insulting love poems to the Muslim women, always with the intent of causing as much disaffection as possible. At last Mahomet waxed impatient and cried:

"Who will give me peace from this Ka'b al' Ashraf?"

Mahomet Mosleima replied, "I, even I will slay him."

The method of his accomplishment of this deed is instructive of the estimation in which individual life was then held. Mosleima secured the assistance of Ka'b's treacherous brother—how, we are not told, but most probably by bribes. Together the two went to the poet's house by moonlight, and begged his company on a discussion of much importance. His young wife would have prevented Ka'b, sensing treachery from the manner and time of the request, but he disregarded her prayers. In the gleam of moonbeams the three walked past the outskirts of the city in deepest converse, the subject of which was rebellion against the Prophet.

They came at length to the ravine Adjuz, a lonely place overhung with ghastly silence and pallid under the white light. Here they stopped, and soon his brother began to stroke the hair of Ka'b until he had lulled him into drowsiness. Then suddenly seizing the forelock he shouted:

"Let the enemy of God perish!"

Ka'b was pinioned, while four men of the Beni Aus slashed at him with their swords. But he was a brave man and strong, determined to sell his life dearly. The struggle became furious.

"When I saw that," relates Mosleima through the mouth of tradition, "I remembered my dagger, and thrust it into his body with such violence that it penetrated the entire bulk. The enemy of God gave one cry and fell to the ground."

Then they left him, and hastened to tell their master of the good news. Mahomet rejoiced, and was at no pains to conceal his satisfaction. Ka'b had made himself objectionable to the Prophet and dangerous to Islam; Ka'b was removed; it was well; Allah Akbar Islam.

Eastern nations have never been so careful of human life as Western, and especially as the Anglo-Saxon peoples. To Mahomet the security of his state came before all, and if a hundred poets had threatened to undermine his authority, he would have had them all slain with equal steadfastness. Men were bound to die, and those who disturbed the progress of affairs merely suffered more swiftly the universal lot. It is obvious that no modern Western standard can be set up for Mahomet; the deed must be interpreted by that inflexible will and determination to achieve his aims, which lies at the root of all his crimes of state. But the unfortunate Jews went in fear and trembling, and their panic was increased when Mahomet issued an order to his followers with permission to kill them wherever they might be found. He very soon, however, allowed so drastic a command to lapse, but not before some had taken advantage of his savage policy, and after a time he made a new treaty with the Jews, not at all on the old federal lines, but guaranteeing them some sort of security, provided they showed proper submission to his superior power. This treaty smoothed over matters somewhat, but nevertheless the Jews were now thoroughly intimidated, and those who were left lived a restricted life, wherein fear played the greater part.

But for the time being Mahomet was satisfied, and no further punitive acts were attempted; not many months later he was faced with a far greater danger, the appearance in force of his old enemy the Kureisch, burning for vengeance, fierce in their hatred of such a despoiler, and before them Mahomet in the new-found arrogance of his dominion was forced to pause.

CHAPTER XIII

THE BATTLE OF OHOD

"If a wound hath befallen you, a wound like it hath already befallen others; we alternate these days (of good and evil fortune) among men, that God may know those who have believed and that He may take martyrs from among you."—*The Kuran*.

The Jews had been alternately forced and cajoled into submission, the Disaffected had been swept into temporary loyalty after the triumph at Bedr, his own followers were magnificently proud of his dominance, the Kureisch had made as yet no serious endeavours to avenge their humiliation at Bedr; moreover, the religious and political affairs of the city had been regulated so that it was possible to carry on the usual business of life in security—a security which certainly possessed no guaranteed permanence, and which might at any moment crack beneath the feet of those who walked thereon and plunge them back into an anarchy of warring creeds and chiefs— still a security such as Medina had seldom known, built up by the one strong personality within its walls.

For a few months Mahomet could live in peace among his followers, and the interest shifts not to his religious ordinances and work of government—these had been successfully started, and were now continuing almost automatically—but to his domestic life and his relations with his intimate circle of friends. As his years increased he felt the continual need of companionship and consolation, and while he sought for advice in government and counsel in war from such men as Abu Bekr, Ali, and Othman, he found solace and refreshment in the ministering hands of women.

Sawda he already possessed, and her slow softness and unimaginative mind had already begun to pall; Ayesha, with her beauty and shrewdness, her jewel-like nature, bright and almost as hard, could lessen the continual strain of his life, and induce by a kind of reflex action that tireless energy of mind find body which was the secret of his power. But these were not enough, and now he sought fresh pleasure in Haphsa, and in other and lesser women, though he never cast away his earlier loves, still with the same unformulated desire, to obtain some respite from the cares which beset him, some renewal of his vivid nature, burning with self-destroying fire.

The emotional stimulus, whose agents women were, became for him as necessary as prayer, and we see him in later life adding experience after experience in his search for solace, nevertheless cleaving most to Ayesha, whose vitality fulfilled his intensest need. Secondary to the necessity of refreshment came the not inconsiderable duty of securing the permanence of his power by the foundation of a line of male successors. His earlier marriages had been productive only of daughters, while his later unions, and also his most recent with Haphsa, had been unfruitful. But though so far no direct male issue had been vouchsafed him, he was careful to unite with himself the most important men in his state by marriage with his children, binding them thereby with the closest blood ties. Rockeya, now dead, had married the warrior Othman, and Fatima, the Prophet's youngest daughter, was bestowed upon the bright and impetuous Ali, whose exploits in warfare had filled the Muslim with pride and a wondering fear. Of this marriage were born the famous Hassan and Hosein, names written indelibly upon the Muslim roll of fame.

As each inmate became added to his household, rough houses, almost huts, were built for their reception, but the Prophet himself had no abiding place, only a council-chamber, where he conducted public business, and dwelt by turn in the houses of his wives, but delighted most to visit Ayesha, who occupied the foremost position by virtue of her beauty and personality. Mahomet's household grew up gradually near the Mosque in this manner; together with the houses of his sons-in-law, not far away, and the sacred place itself, it constituted the centre of activity for the Muslim world, witnessing the arrival and despatch of embassies, the administration of justice and public business, the performance of the Muslim religious ceremonial, the Kuranic revelations of Allah's will. It radiated Mahomet's personality, and concentrated for his followers all the enthusiasm and persistence that had gone to its creation, as well as the endurance and foresight ensuring its continuance.

But such security was not permanently possible for Mahomet; his spirit was doomed to perpetual sojourn amid tumult and effort. It was almost twelve months since the victory of Bedr. The broken Kureisch had had time to recover themselves, and they were now prepared for revenge. The wealth of Abu Sofian's caravan, so dearly acquired, had not been distributed after Bedr. It remained inviolate at Mecca, a weapon wherefrom was to be wrought their bitter vengeance. All their fighting men were massed into a great host. Horses and armour, weapons and trappings were bought with their hoarded wealth, and at length, 3000 strong, including 700 mailed warriors and 200 well-mounted cavalry, they prepared to set forth upon their work of punishment.

Not only were their own citizens pressed into the service, but the fighting men from allied neighbouring tribes, who were very ready to take part in an expedition that promised excitement and bloodshed, with the hope of plunder. The wives of their chief men implored permission to go with the army, pointing out their usefulness and their great eagerness to share the coming triumph. But many warriors murmured against this, for the undertaking was a difficult one, and they knew the discomforts of a long march. At length fifteen specially privileged women were allowed to travel with the host, among them Hind, the fierce wife of Abu Sofian, who brought in her train an immense negro, specially reserved for her crowning act of vengeance, the murder of Hamza, in revenge for the slaying of her father. The army took the easier seaward route, travelling as before in all the pomp and gorgeousness of Eastern warfare, and finally reached the valley of Akik, five miles west of Medina. Thence they turned to the left, so as to command a more vulnerable place in the city's defences, and finally encamped at Ohod at the base of the hill on a fertile plain, separated from the city to the north by several rocky ridges, impassable for such an army.

Mahomet's first news of the premeditated attack reached him through his uncle Abbas, that weak doubter, who never could make up his mind to become either the friend or the foe of Islam. He sent a messenger to Coba to say that the Kureiseh were advancing in force. Mahomet was inevitably the leader of the city in spite of the bad feeling between himself and certain sections within it. Jews and Disaffected alike looked to him for leadership in such a crisis; by virtue of his former prowess his counsels were sought.

Mahomet knew perfectly well that this attacking force was unlike the last, which had been gathered together hurriedly and had underestimated its opposition. He knew that besides a better equipment they possessed the strongest incentive to daring and determination, the desire to avenge some wrong. It was with no false estimate of their foe that he counselled his followers to remain in their city and allow the enemy to waste his strength on their defences. Abdallah agreed with the Prophet's decision, but the younger section, and especially those who had not fought at Bedr, were clamorously dissentient. They pointed out that if Mahomet did not go forth to meet the Kureisch he would lay himself open to the charge of cowardice, and they openly declared that their loyalty to the Prophet would not endure this outrage, but would turn to contempt. Against his will Mahomet was forced into action. He might succeed in defeating his foe, and at all events his position would not endure the disloyalty and disaffection that his refusal would entail.

After Friday's service he retired to his chamber, and appeared before the people in armour. He called for three lances and fixed his banners to them, designing one for the leaders of the refugees, and the other two for the tribes of the Beni Aus and Khazraj. He could muster in this year an army of 1000 men, but he had no cavalry, and fewer mailed warriors than the Kureisch. Abdallah tried his best to dissuade Mahomet, but the Prophet was firm.

"It does not become me to lay aside my armour when once I have put it on, without meeting my foe in battle."

At dawn the army moved to Ohod, and he drew up his line of battle at the base of the hill directly facing the Kureisch. But before he could take up his final position, Abdallah with three hundred men turned their backs upon him and hastened again to Medina, declaring that the enterprise was too perilous, and that it had been undertaken against their judgment. Mahomet let them go with the same proud sufficiency that he had showed before the advancing host at Bedr.

"We do not need them, the Lord is on our side."

Then he directed his attention to the disposition of his forces. He stationed fifty archers under a captain on the left of his line, with strict orders that they were to hold their ground whatever chance befell, so as to guard his rear and foil a Kureischite flank movement. Then, having provided for the enemy's probable tactics, he drew out his main line facing Medina in rather shallow formation.

The attack began as usual, by single combats, in which none of the champions seem to have taken part, and soon Mahomet's whole line was engaged in a ruthless onward sweep, before which the Kureisch wavered. But the Muslim pressed too hotly, and unable to retain their ground at all points, were driven back here and there. Again their long line recovered and pursued its foes, only to lose its coherence and discipline; for a section of them, counting the day already won, began plundering the Kureisch camp. This was too much for the archers on the left.

Forgetting everything in one wild desire to share the enemy's wealth, they left their post and charged down into the struggling central mass.

Here was Khalid's chance. The chief warrior and counsellor of the Kureisch gathered his men together hastily, and circling round the now oblivious Muslim, drove his force against their rear, which broke up and fled. Mahomet instantly saw the fatal mistake, and commanded the archers across the sea of men and weapons to remember their orders and stand firm. But it was too late, and all he could do was to attempt to stay the Muslim flight.

"I am the Apostle of God, return!" he called across the tumult.

But even his magnetism failed to rally the stricken Muslim, and they rushed in headlong flight towards the slopes of Ohod. In the chaos that followed, Hind saw her enemy standing against the press of his fellow-citizens, striving to encourage them, while with his sword he cut at the pursuing Kureisch. She sent her giant negro, Wahschi, to cleave his way to the abhorred one through the struggling men, and he crashed them asunder with spear uplifted to strike. Hamza was felled to the ground, and with one despairing upward thrust, easily parried by his huge assailant, he succumbed to Wahschi's spear and lay lifeless, the first martyr in the cause of Islam, which still remembers with pride his glorious end.

Seven refugees and citizens gathered round their leader to defend him, but the battle raged in his vicinity, and his friends could not keep off the blows of his enemies. He was wounded, and some of his teeth were knocked out. Then the cry arose that he was slain, and the evil tidings heightened the Muslim disaster. A wretched remnant managed to gain the security of the hill slopes, and not the good news of Mahomet's escape when they saw him amongst them could make of them aught but a vanquished and ignominious band. They lay hidden among the hills, while the Kureisch worked their triumphant vengeance upon the corpses of their victims, which they mutilated before burying, after the barbarous fashion of the time, and the savage wrath of Hind found appeasement in her destruction of Hamza's body. At length the Kureisch prepared to depart, and their spokesman, going to the base of the fatal hill, demanded the Prophet's agreement to a fresh encounter in the following year. Omar consented on behalf of the Prophet and his followers, and Mahomet remained silent, wishing to confirm the impression that he was dead.

Why the Kureisch did not follow up their victory and attempt a raid upon Medina, it is difficult to imagine. Possibly they were apprehensive that Mahomet might have fresh reserves and strong defences within the city; but more probably they felt they had accomplished their purpose and the Muslim would now be cured of seeking to plunder their caravans. So they retreated again towards Mecca, and the forlorn Muslim crept silently from their hiding-places to discover the extent of their defeat. They found seventy-four bodies of their own following and twenty of the enemy. Their ignominy was complete, and to the bitterness of their reverse was added the terrible fear that the Kureisch would proceed further and attack their defenceless city.

They returned to Medina at sunset, a mournful and piteous band, bearing with them their leader, whose wounds had been hastily dressed on the field. Mahomet was indeed in sore straits; himself maimed, the bulk of his army scattered, his foes victorious and his headquarters full of seething discontent, brought to the surface by his defeat, he felt himself in peril even at Medina, and passed the night fearfully awaiting what events might bring fresh disaster. But his determination and foresight did not desert him, and once the tormenting night was passed he recovered his old resourcefulness and his wonderful energy.

He commanded Bilal to announce that he would pursue the Kureisch, and put himself, stricken and suffering, at the head of the expedition. They reached Safra, and remained there three days, returning then to Medina with the announcement that the Kureisch had eluded them. This sortie was nothing more than a manifestation of courage, and by it Mahomet hoped to restore in a measure his shaken confidence in the city, and also to apprise the Kureisch that he was not utterly crushed.

But his defeat had damaged his prestige far more than a mere expedition could remedy, and his followers were aghast at his humiliation. Their world was upturned. It was as if the Lord Himself, for whom they had suffered so much, had suddenly demonstrated His frailty and human weakness. And the malcontents in Medina triumphed, especially the Jews, who saw with joy some measure of the Prophet's brutality towards them being meted to him in turn. The situation was grave, and Mahomet's reputation must be at all costs re-established. He retired for some time to his own quarters, and received the revelation of part of Sura iii, wherein he explains the whole matter, urging first that Allah was pleased to make a selection between the brave and the cowardly, the weak and the steadfast, and then that the defeat was the punishment for disobeying his divine commands. The passage is written in Mahomet's most forcible style, and stands out clearly as a reliable account, for neither the defeat of the Muslim, nor their own culpability, are minimised. The martyrs at Ohod receive at his hands their crown of praise.

"And repute not those slain on God's path to be dead. Nay, alive with their Lord are they, and richly sustained. Rejoicing in what God of His bounty hath vouchsafed, filled with joy at the favours of God, and at His mercy; and that God suffereth not the reward of the faithful to perish."

He spends most time, however, in speaking for the encouragement of his sorely tried flock, and for the confusion of those who doubt him. The revelation came in answer to a direct need, and is inseparable from the events which called it forth.

As far as was possible it achieved its purpose, for the Faithful received it with humility, but it could not fully restore the shaken confidence in the Prophet.

The immediate result of the battle of Ohod was to render Mahomet free from any more threatenings from the Kureisch, who had fulfilled the task of overawing him into quietude towards them, but its ultimate results were far-reaching and endured for many years; in fact, it was by reason of the reverse at Ohod that the next period of his life is crowded with defensive and punitive expeditions, and attacks upon his followers by desert tribes. His position at Medina had been rendered thoroughly insecure, and every tribe deemed it possible to accomplish some kind of demonstration against him. Jew and Arabian both pitted themselves against the embryo state, and the powerful desert allies of the Kureisch constituted a perpetual menace to his own stronghold. It was only when he had murdered or exiled every Jew, and carried out repeated campaigns against the tribes of the interior, that his position in Medina was removed beyond possibility of assailment.

Ruthlessness and trust in the sword were his only chances of success. If he relaxed his vigilance or allowed any humane feelings to prevent the execution of severe measures upon any of his enemies, his very existence would be menaced. From now he may be said to pass under the tyranny of war, and its remorseless urging was never slackened until he had his own native city within his power. The god of battles exacted his pitiless toll from his devotee, compelling him to work out his destiny by the sword's rough means. The thinker has become irrevocably the man of action; prayer has been supplemented by the command, "Fight, and yet again fight, that God may conquer and retain." Reverses show the temper of heroes, and Mahomet is never more fully revealed than in the first gloomy days after Ohod, when he steadfastly set himself to retrieve what was lost, refusing to acknowledge that his position was impaired, impervious to the whispers that spoke of failure, supreme in his mighty asset of an impregnable faith.

CHAPTER XIV

THE TYRANNY OF WAR

"And we have sent down Iron. Dire evil resideth in it, as well as advantage to mankind."—*The Kuran.*

After the battle of Ohod, two months passed quietly for Mahomet. He was unable to undertake any aggressive expeditions, and both the Jews at Medina and the exterior desert tribes were lulled into tranquillity by the knowledge that his power was for the time considerably weakened. But the Prophet knew that this security could not continue for long, and for the character of his future wars he was fully prepared—sufficient proof, if one were still necessary, of his skill as soldier and leader.

He knew the Kureisch had instituted a policy of alliance with the surrounding tribes, and that now their plan would be to crush him by a ceaseless pressure from the east, united to the inevitable disaffection within the city as its inhabitants witnessed the decline of their leader's power. Watchfulness and severity were the only means of holding his position, and these two qualities he used with a tenacity which alone secured his ultimate success.

The first threatenings came from the Beni Asad, a powerful tribe inhabiting the country directly east of Medina. Under their chief Tuleiha, they planned a raid against Mahomet. But his excellent system of espionage stood him, now as always, in good stead, so that he heard of their scheme before it was ripe, and despatched 150 men to frustrate it. The Beni Asad were wise enough to give up the attempt after Mahomet's men had found and plundered their camp. They dispersed for the time being, and the danger of an attack was averted. But scarcely had the expedition returned when news came of another gathering at Orna, between Mecca and Taif. Again Mahomet lost no time, but sent a force large enough to disperse them in a skirmish, in which the chief of the Lahyan tribe was killed.

In the next month Mahomet sent six of his followers to Mecca, probably as spies, but they were not allowed to reach their goal in safety. At Raja they fell in with a party of the Beni Lahyan proceeding the same way. The men were armed, and Mahomet's followers were glad to accompany them, because of the additional security. At the oasis the party encamped for the night, and the Muslim prepared unsuspectingly for sleep. At dead of night they were surrounded by their professed friends, who were resolved on revenge for the murder of their chief. Four were killed, and two, Zeid and Khubeib, taken bound to Mecca, whose citizens gloated over their prey. Legends in plenty group themselves around these two figures—the first real martyrs for Islam, and one of the most profound testimonies to the love which Mahomet inspired in his followers is given traditionally in a few significant sentences dealing with the episode.

The prisoners were kept a month before being led to the inevitable torture. Abu Sofian, the scoffer, came to Zeid as he was preparing to face his death.

"Wouldst thou not, O Zeid," he asked, "that thou wert once more with thy family, and that Mahomet suffered in thy place?"

"By Allah! I would not that Mahomet should suffer the smallest prick from a thorn; no, not even if by that means I could be safe once more among my kindred."

Then the enemy of Islam marvelled at his words and said: "Never have I seen among men such love as Mahomet's followers bear towards him."

And after that Zeid was put to death. Mahomet was powerless to retaliate, and was obliged to suffer from afar the murder of his fellow-believers.

The fate of these six Muslim gave courage to Mahomet's enemies everywhere, and prompted even his friends to treachery. The Beni Aamir, a branch of the great Hawazin tribe dwelling between the Beni Asad and the Beni Lahyan, were friendly towards Medina, and sent Mahomet gifts as a guarantee. These Mahomet refused to receive unless the tribe became converts to Islam. He knew the danger of compromise—his Meccan experiences had not faded from his mind; moreover, he recognised that in his present weakened position firmness was essential. He could not open the gates of his fortress even a chink without letting in a flood before which it must topple into ruin.

But their chief would not be so coerced, neither would he give up his ancestral faith without due examination of that offered in its stead. He demanded that a party of Muslim should accompany him back to his own people and strive by reasoning and eloquence to convert them to Islam. After much deliberation, for he was chary of sending any of his chosen to what would be swift death in the event of treachery, Mahomet consented, and gave orders for a party of men skilled in their faith to accompany Abu Bera back to his people. The men were received in all honour, and were escorted as befitted their position as far as Bir Mauna, where they halted, and a Muslim messenger was sent with a letter to the chief of another branch of the same tribe. This leader, Aamir ibn Sofail, immediately put the messenger to death, and called upon his allies to exterminate the followers of the blasphemous Prophet. But the tribe refused to break Abu Bera's pledge, so Aamir, determined to root them out, appealed to the Beni Suleim, Mahomet's avowed enemies, and with their aid proceeded to Bir Mauna. There they fell upon the band of Muslim and slaughtered them to a man, then returned to their desert fastnesses, proudly confident in their ability to elude pursuit. The news was carried to Mahomet, and at first he was convinced that Abu Bera had betrayed him. His followers, who had brought the news, had fallen upon and killed some luckless members of the Beni Aamir in reprisal, and Mahomet acclaimed their action. When, however, he heard from Abu Bera that he and his tribe had been faithful to their pledge, he paid blood money for the murdered men; then calling his people together he solemnly cursed each tribe by name who had dared to attack the Faithful by treachery.

But the incident did not end here. Mahomet could not compass the destruction of the Beni Aamir; they were too powerful and dwelt too far off for his vengeance to assail them, but the Beni Nadhir, the second Jewish tribe within the Prophet's territory, were near, and they were confederate with the treacherous people. Mahomet's action was swift and effective. Force was his only temporal weapon; compulsion his only policy.

The command went forth through the lips of Mosleima:

"Thus saith the Prophet of the Lord: Ye shall go forth out of my land within a space of ten days; whosoever that remaineth behind shall be put to death."

The Beni Nadhir were aghast and trembling. They urged their former treaties with Mahomet, and the antiquity of their settlements. It was impossible that they should break up their homesteads thus suddenly and depart forlorn into an unknown land. But Mahomet was obdurate, with that same fixity of purpose which was everywhere the keynote of his dominance.

"Hearts are changed now," was the only reply to their prayers, their entreaties, and their throats. Abdallah, leader of the Beni Aus and Khazraj, sought desperately for a reconciliation, but to no purpose; the die was cast. Then the Jews, brought to bay and careless with the despair of impotence, refused to obey the command, and prepared to encounter the wrath of Allah and the vengeance of his emissary.

"Behold the Jews prepare to fight: great is the Lord!" the Prophet declared when the news was brought to him.

He was sure of his victim, and ruthless in destruction. All things were made ready for the undertaking. The army was assembled and the march begun. Ali carried the great green banner of the Prophet towards the stronghold of his enemies. The Beni Nadhir were invested in their own quarters, the date trees lying outside their fort were burned, their fields were laid waste. For three weeks the siege endured, each day bringing the miserable garrison nearer to the inevitable privations and final surrender. At last the Jews recognised the hopelessness of their lot and came to reluctant terms, submitting to exile and agreeing to depart immediately.

Then followed the terrible breaking up of homes, and the wandering forth of a whole tribe, as of old, to seek other dwelling-places. Some went to Kheibar, where they were to suffer later on still more severely at Mahomet's hands; some went to Jericho and the highlands south of Syria, but all vanished from their ancient abiding places as suddenly as if a plague had reduced their land to silence. It was an important conquest for Mahomet, and has found fitting notice in the Kuran. The number of his enemies within the city was considerably reduced. He was gradually proving his power by breaking up the Jewish federations, and thereby advancing far towards his goal, his unassailable, almost royal dominance of Medina. Moreover, he bound the refugees closer to him by dividing the despoiled country amongst them. It was an event worthy of incorporation into the record of divine favours, for by it the sacred cause of Islam had been rendered more triumphant.

"God is the mighty, the wise! He it is who caused the unbelievers among the people of the Book to quit their homes. And were it not that God had decreed their exile, surely in this world would he have chastised them: but in the world to come the chastisement of the fire awaiteth them. This because they set them against God and His Apostle, and whoso setteth him against God—! God truly is vehement in punishing."

The sura ends in a mood of fierce exultation unrivalled by any ecstatic utterances of his early visions. It is the measure of his relief at his first great success since the humiliation of Ohod. His fervour beats through it like the clamour of waters, in whose triumphant gladness no pauses are heard.

"He is God, beside whom there is no God: He is the King, the Holy, the Peaceful, the Faithful, the Guardian, the Mighty, the Strong, the Most High! Far be the glory of God from that which they unite with Him! He is God, the Producer, the Maker, the Fashioner! To Him are ascribed excellent titles. What ever is in the Heavens and in the Earth praiseth Him. He is the Mighty, the Wise!"

The expulsion of the Beni Nadhir was a brutal, but necessary act. The choice lay between their security and his future dominion, and he uprooted their dwellings as ruthlessly as any conqueror sets aside the obstacles in his path. Half measures were impossible, even dangerous, and Mahomet was not afraid to use terrible means to achieve his all-absorbing end. He had avowedly accepted the behests of the sword, and did not repudiate his master. The hated Jews were enemies of his God, whose vicegerent he now ranked himself; their ruin was in the divinely appointed order of the world.

The time was soon at hand when, by arrangement, the Medinan army was to repair to Bedr to meet the Kureisch. The Meccans sent a messenger in Schaban (Nov. 625) to Mahomet, saying that they were prepared to advance against him with 2000 foot and 50 horse. This large army did in reality set out, but was soon forced to return, owing to lack of supplies and scarcity of food.

The message was sent mainly in the hope of intimidating the Muslim, but Mahomet was probably as well informed of the Kureisch movements as they were themselves, and knew that no real attack was possible. He therefore determined to show both friends and enemies that he was ready to meet his foes. The Muslim were not very agreeable, knowing what fate had decreed at their last encounter with the Meccans, but Mahomet's stern determination prevailed. He declared that he would go to Bedr even if he went alone, and so collected by sheer force of will 1500 men. He marched to Bedr, held camp there for eight days, during which, of course, no demonstration was made, and the whole expedition was turned into a peaceable mercantile undertaking. When all their goods had been profitably sold or exchanged, Mahomet broke up the camp and returned in triumph to Medina. His prestige had certainly been much increased by this unmolested sortie. It was therefore in a glad and confident mood that he returned to his native city and prepared to enjoy his success.

He took thereupon two wives, Zeinab and Omm Salma, of whom very little is known, except that Zeinab was the widow of Mahomet's cousin killed at Bedr. The incident of his marriage with Zeinab finds allusion in the Kuran in the briefest of passages. She was probably taken as much out of a desire to protect as a desire to possess, and she quickly became one of the many with whom Mahomet was content to pass a few days and nights. There are also signs in the Kuran at this time of disagreements between the different members of his household, and of their extravagant demands upon Mahomet.

It was evidently not so easy to rule his wives as to acquire them. Moreover, he was beginning to feel the sting of jealousy towards every other man of the Muslim.

Here really begins the insistence upon restrictive regulations for women which has been ever since the bane of Islam. Mahomet could not allow his wives to go abroad freely, decked in the ornaments he himself had bestowed, to become a mark for every envious gazer. They were not as other women, and his imperious nature regarded them as peculiarly inviolate, so that he fenced in their actions and secluded their lives. As early as his marriage with Zeinab he imposed restrictions upon women's dress abroad. They are not to traverse the streets in jewels or beautiful robes, but are to cover themselves closely with a long sober garment. Whereas his former sura regarding women had been confined to codifying and rendering fairer divorce and property laws, now the personal note sounds strongly, and continues throughout the whole of his later pronouncements, regarding Muslim women. The next few months were to see dangers and disturbances in his domestic life which were to fix the position of women in Islam throughout the coming centuries, but before he had long completed his latest marriage he was called away upon another necessary expedition. Thus casually, almost from purely personal considerations, was the law regarding the status of women established in Islam. His ordinances have the savour of their impetuous creator, who found in the subject sex no opposition against the writing down, in their most sacred book, of those decrees which rendered their inferior position permanent and authorised. It was Allah speaking through the lips of His Prophet, and they submitted with willing hearts with no shadow of the knowledge of all it was to mean to their descendants darkening their minds.

In Muharram of 626 the Beni Ghatafan, always formidable on account of their size and their desert hinterland, assembled in force at Dzat-al-Rica. Mahomet determinedly marched against them, and once more at the news of his approach their courage failed them, and they fled to the mountains. Mahomet came unexpectedly upon their habitations, carried off some of their women as slaves, and returned to Medina after fifteen days, having effectively crushed the incipient rising against him. The event is chiefly important as being the occasion which led Mahomet to institute the Service of Danger described in the Kuran, whereby half the army prayed or slept while the other watched. A body of men was therefore kept constantly under arms while the army was in the field, and public prayers were repeated twice.

"And when ye go forth to war in the land, it shall be no crime in you to cut short your prayers.... And when thou, O Apostle, shalt be among them and shalt pray with them, then let a party of them rise up with thee, but let them take their arms; and when they shall have made their prostrations, let them retire to your rear: then let another party that hath not prayed come forward, and let them pray with you; but let them take their precautions and their arms."

The military organisation is being gradually perfected, so that the Mahometan sword may finally be in the perpetual ascendant. This was the chief significance of a campaign which at best was only an interlude in the daily life of prayer, civil and domestic cares and regulations which took up Mahomet's life in the breathing space before the great Meccan attack.

Mahomet was absent from Medina but fifteen days, and he returned home resolved to take advantage of the respite from war. Not long after his return he happened to visit the house of Zeid, his adopted son, and chanced not on Zeid, but on his wife at her tiring. Mahomet was filled with her beauty, for her loveliness was past praise, and he coveted her. Zeinab herself was proud of the honour vouchsafed her, and was willing, indeed anxious, to become divorced for so mighty a ruler. Zeid, her husband, with that measureless devotion which the Prophet inspired in his followers, offered to divorce her for him. Mahomet at first refused, declaring it was not meet that such a thing should be, but after a time his desire proved too strong for him, and he consented. So Zeinab was divorced, and passed into the harem of the Prophet. And he justified the proceedings in Sura 33:

> "And when Zeid had settled concerning her to divorce her, we married her to thee, that it might not be a crime in the Faithful to marry the wives of their adopted sons, when they have settled the affair concerning them…. No blame attacheth to the Prophet when God hath given him a permission."

There follows the sum of Mahomet's restrictions upon the dress and demeanour of women. They are to veil their faces when abroad, and suffer no man but their intimate kinsmen to look upon them. The Faithful are forbidden to go near the dwelling-places of the Prophet's wives without his permission, nor are they even to desire to marry them after the Prophet is dead. By such casual means, by decrees born out of the circumstances of his age and personal temperament, did Mahomet institute the customs which are more vital to the position and fate of Muslim women than all his utterances as to their just treatment and his injunctions against their oppression.

Power was already taking its insidious hold upon him, and his feet were set upon the path that led to the despotism of the Chalifate and the horrors of Muslim conquests. Allah is still omnipotent, but He is making continual and indispensable use of temporal means to achieve His ends, and His servant does likewise.

After the interlude of peace, Mahomet was called upon in July, 626, to undertake a punitive expedition to Jumat-al-Gandal, an oasis midway between the Red Sea and the Gulf of Persia. The expedition was successful, and the marauders dispersed. He had now reached the confines of

Syria, and, with the extension of his expeditionary activities, his political horizon widened. He began to conceive himself as the predatory chief of Arabia, one who was regarded with awe and fear by the surrounding tribes, with the one exception of the stiff-necked city, Mecca, whose inhabitants he longed in vain to subdue. The success fostered his love of plunder, and inclined him more than ever to hold out this reward of valour to his followers. His stern and wary policy was justified by its success, for by it he had recovered from the severe blow at Ohod, but it threatened to become his master and set its perpetual seal upon his life.

In December, 626, he heard of the defection of the Beni Mustalik, a branch of the Khozaa tribe. They joined the Kureisch for mixed motives, chiefly political, for they hoped to make themselves and their religion secure by alliance with Mahomet's enemies. Mahomet learnt of their desertion through his efficient spies, and determined to anticipate any disturbance. With Ayesha and Omm Salma to accompany him, and an adequate army to support him, he set out for the quarters of the Beni Mustalik, and before long reached Moraisi, where he encamped. The Beni Mustalik were deserted by their allies, and in the skirmish that followed Mahomet was easily successful. Their camp was plundered, their women and some of their men taken prisoner. The expedition was, however, provocative of two consequences which take up considerable attention in contemporary records, the quarrel between the Citizens and the Refugees, and the scandal regarding Ayesha.

The punishment of the Beni Mustalik had been effected, and nought remained but the division of the spoil. The captives had mostly been ransomed, but one, a girl, Juweira, remained sorrowfully with the Muslim, for her ransom was fixed so high that payment was impossible. Mahomet listened to her tale, and the loveliness of her face and figure did not escape him.

"Wilt thou hearken to what may be better?" he asked her, "even that I should pay thy ransom and take thee myself?"

Juweira was thankful for her safety, and rejoiced at her good fortune. Mahomet married her straightway, and for her bridal gift gave her the lives of her fellow tribesmen.

"Wherefore," says Ayesha, "Juweira was the best benefactress to her people in that she restored the captives to their kinsfolk."

But the Citizens and Refugees were by no means so contented. Their quarrel arose nominally out of the distribution of spoil, but really it was a long smouldering discontent that finally burst into flame. Mahomet was faced with what threatened to be a serious revolt, and only his orders for an immediate march prevented the outbreak of desperate passions—greed and envy.

Abdallah, their ubiquitous leader, is chidden in the Kuran, where the whole affair brings down the strength of Mahomet's scorn upon his offending people.

The camp broke up immediately, and through its hasty departure Ayesha was faced with what might have been the tragedy of her life. Her litter was carried away without her by an oversight on the part of the bearers, and she was left alone in the desert's velvet dusk with no alternative but to await its return. The dark deepened, adding its mysterious vastness and silence to trouble her already tremulous mind. In the first hours of the night Safwan, one of Mahomet's rear, came towards her as she sat forlorn, and was amazed to find the Prophet's wife in such a position. He brought his mule near her, then turned his face away as she mounted, so as to keep her inviolate from his gaze. Closely veiled, and trembling as to her meeting with Mahomet, Ayesha rode with Safwan at her bridle until the next day they came up with the main column.

Now murmurs against her broke out on all sides. Mahomet refused to believe her story, and remained estranged from her until she asked permission to return to her father as her word was thus doubted. Ali was consulted by the Prophet, and he, with that antagonism towards Ayesha which germinated later into open hatred, was inclined to believe her defamers. At last the outcry became so great that Mahomet called upon Allah. Entering his chamber in Medina, he received the signs of divine inspiration. When the trance was over, he declared that Ayesha was innocent, and revealed the passage dealing with divorce in Sura 24:

"They who defame virtuous women and bring not four witnesses, scourge them with fourscore stripes, and receive ye not their testimony forever, for these are perverse persons.... And they who shall accuse their wives, and have no witnesses but themselves, the testimony of each of them shall be a testimony by God four times repeated, that He is indeed of them that speak the truth."

The revelation ends with a repetition of the restrictions imposed upon women and an injunction to the Muslim not to enter each other's houses until they have asked leave. This was a necessary ordinance in that primitive community, where bolts were little used and there was virtually no privacy, and was designed, in common with most of his present utterances, to encourage the leading of decent, well-regulated lives by the followers of so magnificent a faith. Ayesha's defamers were publicly scourged, and the matter dismissed from the Muslim mind, save that regulations had once more been framed upon personal feelings and specific events, and were to constitute the whole future law regarding an important and difficult question.

Mahomet was justly content with the position of affairs after the dispersion of the Beni Mustalik. He had shown his strength to the surrounding desert tribes; by systematically crushing each rebellion as it arose, he had demonstrated to them the impossibility of alliance against him. He knew they were each prone to self-seeking and distrustful of each other, and he played unhesitatingly upon their jealousies and passions. Thus he kept them disunited and fearful, afraid even to ally with his powerful enemy the Kureisch. For after all, the Meccans were his chief obstacle; their opposition was spirited and urged on by the memory of past humiliations and triumphs. They alone were really worthy of his steel, and he knew that, as far as the intermediary wars were concerned, they were but the prelude to another encounter in the year-long warfare with his native city.

The drama closes in now upon the protagonists; save for the expulsion of the last Jewish tribe in the neighbourhood of Medina, there is little to compare with that central causal hatred. The final hour was not yet, but the struggle grew in intensity with the passage of time—the struggle wherein one fought for revenge and future freedom from molestation, but the other for the establishment of a faith in its rightful environment, the manifestation before men of that Faith's determined achievement, the symbol of its destined conquests and divinely appointed power.

CHAPTER XV

THE WAR OF THE DITCH

> "And God drove back the Infidels in their wrath; they won no advantage; God sufficed the Faithful in the fight, for God is strong, mighty."—*The Kuran.*

The Kureischite plans for the annihilation of Mahomet were now complete. They had achieved an alliance against him not only among the Bedouin tribes of the interior, but also among the exiled and bitterly vengeful Medinan Jews. Now in Schawwal, 627, Mahomet's unresting foes summoned all their confederates to warfare "against this man." The allied tribes, chief among whom were the Beni Suleim and Ghatafan, always at feud with Mahomet, hastened to mass themselves at Mecca, where they were welcomed confidently by the Kureiseh.

The host was organised in three separate camps, and Abu Sofian was placed at the head of the entire army. Each leader, however, was to have alternating command of the campaign; and this primitive arrangement—the only one, it seems, by which early nations, lacking an indisputable leader, can surmount the jealousy and self-will displayed by every petty chief—is responsible in great measure for their ultimate failure. In such fashion, still with the bravery and splendour of Eastern warfare wrapped about them, an army of 4000 men, with 300 horses, 1500 camels, countless stores, spears, arrows, armour and accoutrements, moved forward upon the small and factious city of the Prophet, whose fighting strength was hampered by the exhaustion of many campaigns and the disloyalty of those within his very walls.

The Prophet was outwardly undismayed; whatever fears preyed upon his inner mind, they were dominated by his unshakable belief in the protection and favour of Allah. He did not allow the days of respite to pass him idly by. As soon as he received the news of this fateful expedition, he called together a meeting of his wisest and bravest, and explained to them the position. He told them of the hordes massed against them, and dwelt upon the impossibility of opposing them in the open field and the necessity of guarding their own city. This time there were no dissentient voices; both the Disaffected and the Muslim had had a lesson at Ohod that was not lightly forgotten. Then Salman, a Persian, and one skilled in war, suggested that their stronghold should be further defended by a trench dug at the most vulnerable parts of the city's outposts.

Medina is built upon "an outcropping mass of rock" which renders attack impossible upon the north-west side. Detached from it, and leaving a considerable vacant space between, a row of compactly built houses stood, making a very passable stone wall defence for that portion of the city. The trench was dug in that level ground between the rocks and the houses, and continued also upon the unsheltered south and east sides. There are many legends of the digging of the trench and the desperate haste with which it was accomplished. Mahomet himself is said to have helped in the work, and it is almost certain that here tradition has not erred. The deed coincides so well with his eager and resolute nature, that never neglected any means, however humble, that would achieve his purpose. The Faithful worked determinedly, devoting their whole days to the task, and never resting from their labours until the whole trench was dug. The hard ground was softened by water, and legendary accounts of Mahomet's powers in pulverising the rocks are numerous.

The great work was completed in six days, and on the evening of its achievement the Muslim army encamped between the trench and the city in the open space thus formed. A tent of red leather was set up for Mahomet, where Zeinab and Omm Salma, as well as his favourite and companion, Ayesha, visited him in turn. Around him rested his chief warriors, Ali, Othman, Zeid, Omar, with his counseller Abu Bekr and his numerous entourage of heroes and enthusiasts. They were infused with the same exalted resolve as their leader, and waited undismayed for the Infidel attack. But with the rest of the citizens, and especially with the Disaffected, it was otherwise. Ever since the rumour of the onrush of their foe reached Medina, they had murmured openly against their leader's rule. They had refused to help in the digging of the ditch, and now waited in ill-concealed discontent mingled with a base panic fear for their own safety.

The Meccan host advanced as before by way of Ohod, and pursued their way to the city rejoicing in the freedom from attack, and convinced thereby that their conquest of Medina would be rapid and complete. They penetrated to the rampart wall of houses and marched past them to the level ground, intending to rush the city and pen the Muslim army within its narrow streets, there to be crushed at will by the sheer mass of its foes. Then as the whole army in battle array moved forward, strong in its might of numbers, the advance was checked and thrown into confusion by the opposing trench. Abu Sofian, hurrying up, learnt with anger of this unexpected barrier. Finding he could not cross it, he waxed indignant, and declared the device was cowardly and "unlike an Arab." The traditionalist, as usual, was disconcerted by the resourceful man of action, and the Muslim obstinately remained behind their defence.

The Kureisch discharged a shower of arrows over the ditch among the entrenched Muslim and then retired a little from their first position, so as to encamp not far from the city and try to starve it into surrender. Mahomet was content that he had staved off immediate attack, and set to work to complete his defences and strengthen his fighting force, when grave news reached him from the immediate environs of the city. Successful as he had been in extirpating two of the hated Jewish tribes, Mahomet was nevertheless forced to submit to the presence of the Beni Koreitza, whose fortresses were situated near the city on its undefended side. It is uncertain whether there was ever a treaty between this tribe and the Prophet, or what its provisions were supposing such a document to have existed, but it is evident that there must have been some peaceable relations between the Muslim and the Koreitza, and that the latter were of some account politically. Now, the Jewish tribe, resentful at the treatment of their fellow-believers, and seeing the t me ripe for secession to the probable winning side, cast away even their nominal allegiance to Mahomet and openly joined his enemies. A Muslim spy was sent to their territory to discover their true feeling, and his report was so disquieting that the Prophet immediately set a guard over his tent, fearing assassination, and ordered patrols to keep the Medinan streets free from any attempts to disturb the peace and threaten his army from within the city's confines.

The Muslim were now in parlous state. The trench might avail to stop the enemy for a time, but an opportunity was sure to occur when they would attempt a crossing, and once within the city Mahomet knew they would carry destruction before them, and irretrievable ruin to his cause. His Jewish enemies made common enmity against him with the Kureisch, and the Disaffected declared their intention of joining the rest of his foes. But he would not yield, and continued unabashed to defend the trench and city with all the skill and energy he could command from his harassed followers.

The Kureisch remained several days inactive, but at last Abu Jahl discovered a weak spot in his enemies' line where the trench was narrow and undefended. He determined on immediate attack, and sent a troop of horsemen to clear the ditch and give battle on the opposite side. The move was noticed from within the defence. Ali and a body of picked men were sent to frustrate it. Ali reached the ground just as the foremost of the Kureisch cleared the ditch and prepared to advance upon the city. Swiftly he leapt from his horse, and challenged an aged chief of the Kureisch to single combat. The gage was accepted, but the chieftain could stand up to Ali no better than a reed stands upright before the wind that shakes it. The chief was slain before the eyes of his friend, and thereupon the general onslaught began. The Muslim fought like those possessed, until in a little space there remained not one of the defiant party that had recently crossed the gulf between the armies. But the Kureisch were undaunted; the order for a general attack upon the trench was now ordered. The assault began in the early morning and continued throughout the day. For long weary hours, without respite and with very little sustenance the Muslin army kept the Kureisch host at bay. The encounters were sharp and prolonged, and none of the men could be spared from the strife to make their daily devotions to Allah.

"They have kept us from our prayers," declared Mahomet in wrath, as he watched the unresting attack, "God fill their bellies and their graves with fire!"

He cursed the Infidel dogs, while exhorting his men to stand firm, and before all things keep their lines unbroken. The attack was repulsed, but not without great loss and misery upon Mahomet's side. His prestige was now entirely lost among the citizens, only the Faithful still rallied round him out of their invincible trust in his personality. The Disaffected began to foment agitation within the narrow streets, the bazaars and public places. There was great distress among the people of Medina; scarcity of food mingled with their fears for the future to create an insecurity wherein crime finds its dwelling-place and brutality its fostering soil. "Then were the Faithful tried, and with strong quaking did they quake." Nevertheless, they stood firm, and took no part in the murmuring of the Disaffected, and presently Allah sent them down succour for their steadfastness and high courage.

Mahomet, failing in direct warfare to drive back his enemies, resorted to strategy. He planned to send a secret embassy to buy off the Beni Ghatafan, and so strive to break up the Kureisch alliance. But the rest of the city were unwilling to adopt this measure, preferring to trust more firmly in the strength of their defences. Finally, Mahomet determined to essay upon his own initiative some means of subtlety whereby he might force back this encompassing foe that hourly threatened his whole dominion. He sent an embassy to the Jews outside the city with intent to sow dissension between them and the Kureisch.

"See now," he commanded his envoy, "whether thou canst not break up this confederacy, for war, after all, is but a game of deception."

The Muslim pursued his way unchecked to the camp of the Koreitza, just outside the city, where he whispered his insidious messages into the ears of the chief, saying the Kureisch were already weary of fighting and were even now planning a retreat, and would forsake their allies as soon as was expedient, leaving them to the mercy of a Muslim revenge. He promised bribes of money, slave girls, and land from the Prophet if they would betray their new-found allies. Self-interest prevailed; at last the plan was agreed upon, and the messenger returned to Mahomet with the good news of the breaking-up of the confederacy.

The treachery of the Koreitza spread discouragement among the Arab chiefs. Moreover, their supplies were already running short. They ceased to press the siege so severely; the attacks became weaker, and Mahomet was easily able to prevent any further incursions beyond the trench. And now the weather broke up. The sunny country was transformed suddenly into a dreary, storm-swept wilderness. Blasts of wind came skurrying down upon the Kureisch camp, driving rain and sleet before them. To Mahomet it was the wrath of the Lord made manifest upon the presumptuous Meccans. Their camp-fires were blown out, their tents damp and draggled, their men dispirited, their forage scarce. Suddenly Abu Sofian, weary of inaction, thoroughly disheartened by the hardships of his position, broke up the camp and ordered a retreat.

The vast army faded away as magically as it had come. The morning after their departure the Muslim awoke to see only a few scattered tents and the disorderly remains of human occupation as evidences of the presence of a foe that had accounted itself invincible. The Meccans evidently accepted defeat, for they returned speedily to their own country, realising bitterly the impossibility of keeping together so heterogeneous an army in the face of a prolonged check. Medina was free of its immediate menace, and great was the rejoicing when the camp was abandoned and Islam returned in security to its sanctuary within the city. Mahomet repaired immediately to Ayesha's house, and was cleansing the stains of conflict from his body when the mandate came from Heaven through the lips of Gabriel:

"Hast thou laid aside thine arms? Lo, the angels have not yet put down their weapons, and I am come to bid thee go against the Beni Koreitza to destroy their citadel."

Mahomet's swift nature, alive to the value of speed, had realised in a flash that now was the time to strike at the Koreitza, the treacherous Hebrew dogs, before they could grow strong and gather together any allies to help them ward off their certain chastisement. The enterprise was proclaimed at once to the weary Muslim, and the great banner, still unfurled, placed in the hands of Ali. The Faithful were eager for rest, but at the command of their leader they forgot their exhaustion and rallied round him again with the same loving and invincible devotion that had sustained them during the terrible days of siege.

The expedition marched to the Koreitza fortress, and laid siege to it in March, 627. For twenty-five days it was besieged by Islam, says the chronicler, until God put terror into the hearts of the Jews, and they were reduced to sore straits. Then they offered to depart as the Kainukaa had departed, empty-handed, with neither gold nor cattle, into a strange land. But Mahomet had not forgotten their treachery to him under the suasion of the Kureisch, and he determined on sterner measures. The Jews were now thoroughly terrified, and sent in haste to crave permission for a visit from Abu Lubaba, an ally of the Beni Aus, their former confederates. Mahomet consented, as one who grants the trivial wish of a doomed man. In sorrow Abu Lubaba went into the camp of the Koreitza, and when they questioned him he told them openly that they must abandon hope. Their doom was decreed by the Prophet, sanctioned by Allah; it was irrevocable.

When the Koreitza heard the sentence they bowed their heads, some in wrath, some in despair, and charged Abu Lubaba with supplications for Mahomet's clemency. The messenger returned and told the Prophet what he had disclosed to the Jews concerning their impending fate.

"Thou hast done ill," declared Mahomet, "for I would not that mine enemies know their doom before it is accomplished."

Thereupon, says tradition, Abu Lubaba was filled with remorse at having displeased his master, and entering the Mosque bound himself to one of its pillars, whence it is called the Pillar of Repentance to this day. At last the Jews, worn out with the siege, without resources, allies, or any hope of relief, surrendered at discretion to the Beni Aus. Immediately their citadel was seized and plundered, while their men were handcuffed and kept apart, their women and children given into the keeping of a renegade Jew. Their cattle were driven into Medina before their eyes, and soon the whole tribe was withdrawn from its ancestral habitation, awaiting what might come from the hand of their terrible foe.

Then Mahomet pronounced judgment. He sent for Sa'ad ibn Muadh, the chief of the Beni Aus, and into his hands he gave the fate of all those souls who belonged to the tribe of Koreitza. Sa'ad was elderly, fat, irritable, and vindictive. He had a long-standing grudge against this people, and knew nothing of the mercy which greater men bestow upon the fallen.

"My judgment is that the men shall be put to death, the women and children sold into slavery, and the spoil divided among the army."

Mahomet was exultant at the sentence.

"Truly the judgment of Sa'ad is the judgment of God pronounced on high from beyond the seventh Heaven."

It accorded with his mood of angry resentment against the earlier treachery of the Koreitza, but why he deputed its pronouncement to Sa'ad instead of taking it upon himself is not easy to discover. Possibly he may have dreaded to acquire such a reputation for cruelty as this would bestow upon him, possibly he wished to make clear to the world that the Jews had been doomed to death by a member of their allied tribe. Certainly he welcomed the terrible sentence, and ensured its accomplishment. The Koreitza were dragged pitilessly to Medina, the men kept together under strict guard, the women and children made ready to be sold at the marts within the city.

That night the outskirts of Medina became the scene of grim activity. In the soft darkness of the Arabian night Mahomet's followers laboured with dreadful haste at the digging of many trenches. The day dawned upon their uncompleted work, and not until the sun was high did they return to the heart of the city. Then the men of the Koreitza were divided into companies and led out in turn to the trenches. The slaughter began. As they filed to the edge of the pits they were struck down by the waiting Muslim, so that their bodies fell into the common grave, mingled with the blood and quivering flesh of those who followed. As one company after another marched out and did not return, their chief man asked the Muslim soldier concerning his countrymen's fate:

"Seest thou not that each company departs and is seen no more? Will ye never understand?"

The doom of the Koreitza was wrought out to its terrible end, which was not until set of sun. The number of butchered men is variously estimated, but it cannot have been less than between 700 and 800.

So the Koreitza perished, each moving forward to meet the irremediable without fear, without supplication, and when the carnage was over, Mahomet turned to the distribution of the spoil. His eyes lighted upon Rihana, a beautiful Jewess, and he desired her as solace after this ruthless but necessary punishment. He offered her marriage; she refused, and became of necessity and forthwith his concubine. Then he took the possessions, slaves, and cattle of the vanquished tribe and divided them among the Faithful, keeping a fifth part himself, and the land he partitioned also. A few women who had found favour in the eyes of Muslim were retained, the rest were sent to be sold as slaves among the Bedouin tribes of Nejd. The Koreitza no longer existed; their treachery had been visited again upon themselves.

The massacre of the Koreitza and the War of the Ditch cannot be viewed apart. The ruthlessness of the former is the outcome of the success which made it possible. Mahomet had defeated a most formidable attempt to overthrow him, an attempt which would have lost much of its potency if the Koreitza had remained either friendly or neutral, and in the triumph which followed he sought to make such treachery henceforth impossible. He never lost an opportunity; he saw that the Koreitza must be dealt with instantly after the failure of the Meccan attack, and unhesitatingly he accomplished his work.

His act is a plain proof of his increasing confidence in his mission and in himself as ruler and emissary from on high. It speaks not only of his barbarity and courage in the use of it when occasion arose, but also of his tireless energy and swift perception of the right moment to strike.

His lack of compunction over the cruelty bears upon it the stamp of his age and environment. The Koreitza were the enemies of Allah and his Prophet; they had dared to betray him. Their doom was just. The result of the failure of the Meccan attack was to restore in great measure Mahomet's reputation, so that he had less trouble hereafter with the Disaffected within Medina and with the maraudings of desert tribes. For the moment his position within the city was comparatively secure; moreover, in exterminating the Koreitza he had removed the last of the hated Hebrew race from the precincts of his adopted city, and could regard himself as master of all its neighbouring territory. The Disaffected, it is true, remained sufficiently at variance with him to resent, though impotently, his severity towards the Koreitza, and to declare that Sa'ad ibn Muadh's death, which occurred soon after, was the direct result of his bloody judgment. But their resentment was confined to speech. The Meccans had retired discredited, and were unlikely to attack again for some time at least.

For a little space Mahomet seemed secure in his city, whence active opposition had been driven out.

The period after the War of the Ditch shows him definitely the ruler of a rival city to Mecca. The Kureisch have made their last concerted attack and are now forced to recognise him as a permanent factor in their political world, though they would not name him equal until he had made further displays of strength. He takes his place now among the city chieftains of Western Arabia, and has next to reckon with the nomad Bedouin tribes of the interior, in which position he is akin to the ruler of Mecca himself. He is still never at rest from warfare. One expedition succeeds another, until there is some chance of the realisation of his dream, whose splendour even now beats with insistence upon his spirit, the establishment of his mighty faith within the mother-city which gave it birth, whence, purged of its idolatries and aflame with devotion, it shall make of that city the goal of its followers' prayers, the crown of its earthly sovereignty.

CHAPTER XVI

THE PILGRIMAGE TO HODEIBIA

"And He it was who held their hands from you and your hands from them in the valley of Mecca, after that He had given you the victory over them; for God saw what ye did."—*The Kuran.*

Mahomet, now secure from immediate attack, counted himself permanently rid of the Meccan menace and devoted his care to the strengthening of his position among the surrounding desert tribes. The year 627-628 is filled with minor expeditions to chastise or conquer his numerous enemies in the interior. His ceaseless vigilance, made effectual through his elaborate spy system, enabled him to keep the Bedouin hordes in check, though he was by no means uniformly successful in his attacks upon them. The period is characterised by the absence of pitched battles, and by the employment of very small raiding parties, who go out simply to plunder and to disperse the hostile forces.

His first expedition after the Koreitza massacre in June 627 was directed against the Beni Lahyan, in revenge for their slaughter of the Faithful at Radji. He took the north-west road to Syria as a feint, then swiftly turning, marched along the sea-shore route to Mecca, and the Beni Lahyan fled before him. Mahomet was anxious to give battle, but as he found his foe was moving hastily towards the hostile city with intent to draw him on to his doom, he gave up the chase and contented himself with breaking up their encampments, plundering their wealth and women, and so returned to Medina.

He had been there only a few nights when he learnt that Oyeina, chief of the Fazara tribe, in concert with the Beni Ghatafan, had made a raid upon his milch camels at Ghaba, killing their keeper and torturing his wife. Mahomet pursued, but the raiders were too quick for him and got away with the spoil. Mahomet did not follow them up, as nothing was to be gained from such a fruitless quest.

In August of the same year another raid on his camels was attempted by the famished tribes of Nejd, and Mahomet sent an expedition under Maslama to chastise them, but the Muslim were overpowered by a superior force and most of their company slain. The Prophet vowed vengeance upon the perpetrators of this defeat when he should have the power to carry it out. And now the Meccan caravan, venturing once more to take the seaward road, so long barred to them, was plundered by Zeid at Al Is, thereby confirming Mahomet's hostile intentions towards the Kureisch, and ensuring their continued enmity. But reprisals on their part were impossible after the failure before Medina, and they suffered the outrage in silence.

Mahomet was not content to rest upon his newly won security, but now determined to send out messengers and embassies to the rulers of surrounding lands, exhorting them to embrace Islam. This policy was to develop later into a regular system, but for the moment only one envoy was sent upon a hazardous mission to the Roman emperor, whose recent conquests in Persia had made him famous among the Arabs. The envoy was not permitted a quiet journey. At Wadi-al-Cora he was seized and plundered by the Beni Judzam, but his property afterwards restored by the influence of a neighbouring tribe allied to Mahomet, who knew something of the revenge meted out by the Prophet. As it was, as soon as he heard of it he despatched Zeid with 500 men, who fell upon the Beni Judzam and slaughtered many. When the expedition returned to Medina with the news, they found that the tribe in question had sent in its submission before the slaying of its members. The Judzam envoys demanded compensation.

"What can be done?" replied Mahomet. "I cannot restore dead men to life, but the booty that has been taken I will return and give you safe escort hence."

Mahomet's next enterprise was to send one of his chief warriors and wise men to Dumah to try and convert the tribe. They listened to his words and promises, and after a time, judging it was not alone to their spiritual, but also to their political welfare to follow this powerful leader, they embraced Islam, and received the protectorship of the Prophet.

Zeid returned from the plunder of the Kureisch caravan and straightway set out upon several mercantile journeys, upon one of which he was set upon and plundered by the Beni Fazara, near Wadi-al-Cora. Swift retribution followed at the hands of Mahomet, who was not minded to see the expeditions that were securing the wealth of his land the prey of marauding tribes. Many barbarities were practised at the overthrow of the Beni Fazara, possibly as a salutary lesson to neighbouring tribes, lest they should presume to attempt like attacks.

But now a further menace threatened Mahomet from the persecuted but still actively hostile Jews at Kheibar. They were suspected of stirring up revolt, and so the Prophet, knowing the activity centred in their leader, slew him by treachery. Still, his successor continued his father's work, only in the fullness of time to be removed from the Prophet's path by the same effectual but illicit means. Dark and tortuous indeed were some of the ways by which Mahomet held his power. His cruelty and treachery were in a measure demanded of him as a necessity for his continued office. They were the price he paid for earthly dominion, and together with the avowed help of the sword they were the stern and pitiless means that secured the triumph of Islam. As time went on the scope of his state-craft widened; its exigencies became more varied, and exacted new and often barbarous deeds, that the position won with years of thought and energy might be maintained. Mahomet has now paid complete homage to the fickle goddesses force and craft.

The sacred month Dzul-Cada of 628 came round, bringing with it disturbing dreams and yearnings for Mahomet. For long past, indeed ever since he had found himself the leader of a religious organisation and had taken the broad traditions of Meccan ceremony half unconsciously to himself as the basis of his faith, he had longed to perform the pilgrimage to the holy city. He had upheld Mecca before the eyes of his followers as the crown and cradle of their faith. He had preached of pilgrimage thereto as a sacred duty, the inalienable right of every Muslim. Six years had elapsed since he had himself performed the sacred rites; it is no wonder, therefore, that his whole being was seized with the fervent dream of accomplishing once more the ceremonies inseparable from his faith. Political considerations also swayed his decision. If he were allowed to come peaceably to Mecca and perform the pilgrimage, it was conceivable that a permanent truce might be agreed upon by the Kureisch, and the deed itself could not but enhance his prestige among the Bedouins. He was strong enough to resist the Meccans in case of an attack, and if such a thing should occur the blame would attach to the Kureisch as violators of the sacred month.

With his thoughts attuned thus, it is not surprising that in Dzul-Cada a vision was vouchsafed him, wherein he saw himself within the sacred precincts, performing the rites of pilgrimage. The dream was communicated to the Faithful, and instant preparations made for the expedition, Mahomet called upon the surrounding tribes to join in his march to Mecca, but they, fearing the Kureisch hosts, for the most part declined, and earned thereby Mahomet's fierce anger in the pages of the Kuran. At length the cavalcade was ready; 1500 men in the garments of pilgrims, but with swords and armour accompanying them in the rear, journeyed over the desert track that had seen the migration to Medina of a small hunted band six short years previously. With them were seventy camels devoted to sacrifice. The pilgrims marched as far as Osfan, when a messenger came to them saying that the Kureisch were opposing their advance.

"They have withdrawn their milch camels from the outskirts, and now lie encamped, having girded themselves with leopard skins, a signal that they will fight like wild beasts. Even now Khalid with their cavalry has advanced to oppose thee."

"Curses upon the Kureisch!" replied Mahomet. "Who will show me a way where they will not meet us?"

A guide was quickly found, and Mahomet turned his company aside, journeying by devious routes until he came to the place of Hodeibia, a plain upon the verge of the sacred territory. Here Al-Cawsa, Mahomet's prized camel, halted, and would in nowise be urged farther.

"She is weary," clamoured the populace, but Mahomet knew otherwise.

"Al-Caswa is not weary," he replied, "but that which restrained the armies in the Year of the Elephant now restraineth her."

And he would go no farther into the sacred territory, fearing the doom that had afflicted Abraha in that fateful year. So his pilgrim host encamped at Hodeibia, and Mahomet sent men to clear the wells of sand and dust, so that there might be ample supply of water. Thereupon negotiations began between the Prophet and Mecca. The Kureisch sent an ambassador to learn the reason of the appearance of Mahomet. When the peaceable intent of the army had been explained to him he remained in earnest converse with the Prophet, until at last he moved to catch at the sacred beard after the manner of his race when speaking. Instantly one of Mahomet's companions seized his hand:

"Come not near the sacred countenance of God's Prophet."

The enemy was amazed, and returning told the citizens that he had seen many kings in his lifetime but never a man so devotedly loved as Mahomet. The negotiations, however, proceeded very tardily, and at last Mahomet sent Othman, his famous warrior and companion, to Mecca to conduct the final overtures. He had been chosen because of his kinship with the most powerful men of Mecca. He was invited to perform the sacred ceremony of encircling the Kaaba, but this he refused to do until the Prophet should accompany him. The Kureisch then detained him at Mecca to complete, if it might be, the negotiations.

While Othman tarried, the report spread among the Muslim that he was treacherously slain. Mahomet felt that a blow had been struck at his very heart. Instantly he summoned the Faithful to him beneath a tall tree upon that undulating plain of Hodeibia, and enjoined upon them an oath that they would not forsake him but would stand by him till death. The Muslim with one accord gave their solemn word in gladness and devotion, and the Pledge of the Tree was brought into being. Mahomet felt the significance of their loyalty very deeply. It was the first oath he had enjoined upon the Believers since the days of the Pledge of Acaba long ago when he was but a persecuted zealot fleeing before the menace of his foes. He was glad because of this proof of loyalty, and his joy finds expression in the Muslim Book of Books:

"Well pleased hath God been now with the Believers when they plighted fealty to thee under the tree; and He knew what was in their hearts; therefore did He send down upon them a spirit of secure repose, and rewarded them with a speedy victory."

But rumour, as ever, proved untrustworthy, and before long Othman returned with the news that the Kureisch were undisposed to battle, and later they sent Suheil of their own clan to make terms with Mahomet, namely, that he was to return to Medina that year, but that the next year he might come again as a pilgrim during the sacred month, and having entered Mecca perform the Pilgrimage. Ali was commanded to write down the conditions of the treaty, and he began with the formula:

"In the name of God, the Compassionate, the Merciful."

Suheil protested, "I know not that title, write, 'In Thy Name, O God.'"

Mahomet acquiesced, and Ali continued, "The Treaty of Mahomet, Prophet of God, with Suheil ibn Amr," but Suheil interrupted again:

"If I acknowledged Thee as Prophet of God I should not have made war on thee; write simply thy name and the name of thy father."

And so the treaty was drawn up. The traditional text of it is simple and clear, and the only point requiring comment is the clause providing for the treatment of those who go over to Islam and those of the Believers who rejoin the Kureisch. Mahomet was sure enough of himself and his magnetism to allow the clause to stand, which allowed any backslider full permission to return to Mecca. He knew there would not be many, who having come under the spell of Islam would return again to idolatry. The text of the treaty stood substantially in these terms:

"In thy Name, O God! These are the conditions of peace between Mahomet, son of Abdallah and Suheil, son of Amr. War shall be suspended for ten years. Whosoever wisheth to join Mahomet or enter into treaty with him shall have liberty to do so; and likewise whoever wisheth to join the Kureisch or enter into treaty with them. If one goeth over to Mahomet without permission of his guardian he shall be sent back to his guardian; but should any of the followers of Mahomet return to the Kureisch they shall not be sent back. Mahomet shall retire this year without entering the city. In the coming year Mahomet may visit Mecca, he and his followers, for three days, during which the Kureisch shall retire and leave the city to them. But they may not enter it with any weapons save those of the traveller, namely, to each a sheathed sword."

After the solemn pledging of the treaty Mahomet sacrificed his victims, shaved his head and changed his raiment, as a symbol of the completed ceremonial in spirit, if not in fact, and ordered the immediate withdrawal to Medina. His followers were crestfallen, for they had been led to expect his speedy entry into Mecca, and they were disappointed too because their warlike desires had been curbed to stifling point. But the Prophet was firm, and promised them fighting in plenty as soon as they should have reached Medina again. So the host moved back to its city of origin, fortified by the treaty with its hitherto implacable foes, and exulting in the promise that next year the sacred ceremonies would be accomplished by all true Believers.

The depression that at first seized his followers at the conclusion of their enterprise found no reflex in the mind of Mahomet. He was well aware of the significance of the transaction. In the Kuran the episode has a sura inspired directly by it and entitled "Victory," the burden of which is the goodness of God upon the occasion of the Prophet's pilgrimage to Hodeibia.

"In truth they who plighted fealty to thee really plighted fealty to God; the hand of God was over their hands! Whoever, therefore, shall break his oath shall only break it to his own hurt; but whoever shall be true to his engagements with God, He will give him a great reward."

It was, in fact, a great step forward towards his ultimate goal. It involved his recognition by the Kureisch as a power of equal importance with themselves. No longer was he the outcast fanatic for whose overthrow the Kureisch army was not required to put forth its full strength. No longer even was he a rebel leader who had succeeded in establishing his precarious power by the sword alone. The treaty of Hodeibia recognises him as sovereign of Medina, and formally concedes to him by implication his temporal governance. It is not to be wondered at, therefore, that his mood on returning to the city was one of rejoicing and praise to Allah who had made such a victory possible.

Henceforward the dream of universal sovereignty took ever more distinctive lineaments in his mind. He pictured first a great and united Arabia, mighty because of its homage to the true God, and supreme because of its birthing of the world-subduing faith. To say that these thoughts had been with him since his first hazardous entry into Medina is to grant him a long-sightedness which his opportunist rule does not warrant. The creator of them was his boundless energy, his force of personality, which kept steadily before him his unquenchable faith and led him from strength to strength. By diplomacy and the sword he had carved out his kingdom, and now he purposed to extend it by suasion and cunning, which nevertheless was to be supported by his soldier's skill and courage. The next phase in his career is one in which reliance is placed as much upon statecraft as warfare, in which he tries with varying success to array his state and his religion along with the great empires and principalities of his Eastern world.

CHAPTER XVII

THE FULFILLED PILGRIMAGE

"O ye to whom the Scriptures have been given! Believe in what we have sent down confirmatory of the Scriptures which is in your hands, ere we efface your features and twist your head round backward, or curse you as we cursed the Sabbath-breakers: and the command of God was carried into effect."

The end of Dzul-Cada saw Mahomet safe in his own city, but with his promises of booty and warfare for his followers unfulfilled. He remained a month at Medina, and then sought means to carry out his pact. He had now determined upon a pure war of aggression, and for this the outcast Jews of Kheibar offered themselves as an acceptable sacrifice in his eyes. In Muharram he prepared an expedition against them, important as being the first of any size that he had undertaken from the offensive. It is a greater proof of his renewed security and rapidly growing power than all the eulogies of his followers and the curses of his enemies. The white standard was placed in the hands of Ali, and the whole host of 1000 strong went up against the fortresses of Kheibar. The Jews were taken completely off their guard. Without allies and with no stores of food and ammunition they could make no prolonged resistance. One by one their forts fell before the Muslim raiders until only the stronghold of Kamuss remained. Mahomet was exultant.

"Allah Akbar! truly when I light upon the coasts of any people, woe unto them in that day."

Then he assembled all his men and put the sacred eagle standard at their head, the white standard with the black eagle embossed, wrought out of the cloak of his wife, Ayesha. He bade them lead the assault upon Kamuss and spare nothing until it should fall to them. In the carnage that followed Marhab, chief of Kheibar, was slain, and at length the Jews were beaten back with terrible loss. There was now no hope left: the fortress Kamuss must fall, and with it the last resistance of the Jews. Their houses, goods, and women were seized, their lands confiscated. Kinana, the chief who had dared to try and originate a coalition previously against Mahomet, was tortured by the burning brand and put to death, while Safia, his seventeen year old bride, passed tranquilly into the hands of the conqueror. Mahomet married her and she was content, indeed rejoiced at this sudden change; for, according to legend, she had dreamed that such honour should befall her.

But all the women of the Jews were not so complacent, and in Zeinab, sister of Marhab, burned all the fierceness and lust for revenge of which the proud Hebrew spirit is capable. She would smite this plunderer of her nation, though it might be by treacherous means. Had he not betrayed her kindred far more terribly upon the bloody slaughter ground of the Koreitza? She prepared for his pleasure a young kid, dressed it with care, and placed it before him. In the shoulder she put the most effective poison she knew, and the rest of the meat she polluted also. When Mahomet came to the partaking he took his favourite morsel, the shoulder, and set it to his lips. Instantly he realised the tainted flavour. He cried to his companions:

"This meat telleth me it is poisoned; eat ye not of it."

But it was too late to save two of the Faithful, who had swallowed mouthfuls of it. They died in tortures a few hours afterwards. Mahomet himself was not immune from its poison. He had himself bled at once, and immediate evil was averted. But he felt the effects of it ever after, and attributed not a little of his later exhaustion to the poisoned meats he had eaten in Kheibar. The woman was put to death horribly, and the Muslim army hastened to depart from the ill-omened place.

They returned to Medina after several months absence, and there the spoil was divided. The land as usual was given out to Muslim followers, or the Jews were allowed to keep their holdings, provided they paid half the produce as tribute to Mahomet. Half the conquered territory, however, was reserved exclusively for the Prophet, constituting a sort of crown domain, whence he drew revenues and profit. Thus was temporal wealth continually employed to strengthen his spiritual kingdom and put his faith upon an unassailable foundation.

The expedition to Kheibar saw the promulgation of several ordinances dealing with the personal and social life of his followers. The dietary laws were put into stricter practice; the flesh of carnivorous animals was forbidden, and a severer embargo was laid upon the drinking of wine—the result of Mahomet's knowledge of the havoc it made among men in that fierce country and among those wild and passionate souls. Henceforward also the most careful count was kept of all the booty taken in warfare, and those who were discovered in the possession of spoil fraudulently obtained were subject to extreme penalties. All spoil was inviolate until the formal division of it, which usually took place upon the battlefield itself or less frequently within Medina. The Prophet's share was one-fifth, and the rest was distributed equally among the warriors and companions. Since Islam derived its temporal wealth chiefly by spoliation, the destiny of its plunder was an important question and gave rise to frequent disputes between the Disaffected and the Believers which are mentioned in the Kuran. By now, however, the malcontents were for the most part silenced, and we hear little disputation after this as to the apportionment of wealth.

With the return to Medina came the inaugury of Mahomet's extension of diplomacy—the dream which had filled his mind since the tide of his fortunes had turned with the Kureisch failure to capture his city. The year 628, the first year of embassies, saw his couriers journeying to the princes and emperors of his immediate world to demand or cajole acknowledgment of his mission. A great seal was engraved, having for its sign "Mahomet, the Prophet of God," and this was appended to the strange and incoherent documents which spread abroad his creed and pretensions.

The first embassy to Heraclius was sent in this year summoning him to follow the religion of God's Prophet and to acknowledge his supremacy. At the same time the Prophet sent a like missive to the Ghassanide prince Harith, ally of Heraclius and a great soldier. The envoys were treated with the contempt inevitable before so strange a request from an unknown fanatic, and Heraclius dismissed the whole matter as the idle word of a barbarian dreamer. But Harith, with the quick resentment harboured by smaller men, asked permission of the Emperor to chastise the impostor. Heraclius refused; the embassy was not worthy of his notice, and he was certainly determined not to lose good fighting men in a useless journey through the desert. So Mahomet received no message in return from the Emperor, but the omission made no difference to his determination to proceed upon his course of diplomacy.

He then sent to Siroes of Persia a similar letter, but here he was treated more rudely. The envoy was received in audience by the king, who read the extraordinary letter and in a flash of anger tore it up. He did not ill-treat the messenger, however, and suffered him to return to his own land.

"Even so, O Lord, rend Thou his kingdom from him!" cried Mahomet as he heard the story of his flouting.

His next enterprise was more successful. The governor of Yemen, Badzan, nominally under the sway of Persia, had separated himself almost entirely from his overlord during the unstable rule of Siroes, son of the warrior Chosroes. Now Badzan embraced Islam, and with his conversion the Yemen population became officially followers of the Prophet. Encouraged by the success, Mahomet sent a despatch to Egypt, where he was courteously received and given two slave girls, Mary and Shirin, as presents. Mary he kept for himself because of her exceeding beauty, but Shirin was bestowed upon one of the Companions. Although the Egyptian king did not embrace Islam, he was kindly disposed towards its Prophet.

The next despatch, to Abyssinia, is distinguished by the importance of its indirect results. Ever since the small body of Islamic converts had fled thither for refuge before the persecutions of the Kureisch, Mahomet had desired to convert Abyssinia to his creed. Now he sent an envoy to its king enjoining him to embrace Islam, and asking for the hand of Omm Haliba in marriage, daughter of Abu Sofian and widow of Obeidallah, one of the "Four Inquirers" of an earlier and almost forgotten time. The despatch was well received by the governor, who allowed Omm Haliba and all who wished of the original immigrants to return to their native country. Jafar, Mahomet's cousin, exiled to Abyssinia in the old troublous times, was the most famous of these disciples. He was a great warrior, and found his glory fighting at the head of the armies of the Prophet at Muta, where he was slain, and entered forthwith upon the Paradise of joy which awaits the martyrs for Islam. Not long after his return from Kheibar the Refugees arrived, and Mahomet took Omm Haliba to wife.

During the remainder of 628 the Prophet held his state in Medina, only sending out some of his lesser leaders at intervals upon small defensive expeditions. His position was now secure, but only just as long as his right arm never wavered and his hands never rested from slaughter. By the edge of the sword his conquests had been made, by the edge of the sword alone they would be kept. But it was now necessary only for him to show his power. The frightened Arab tribes crept away, cowed before his vigilance, but if the whip were once put out of sight they would spring again to the attack.

He now receives the title of Prince of Hadaz, how and by whom bestowed upon him we have no record. Most probably he wrested it himself by force from the tribes inhabiting that country, and compelled them to acknowledge him by that sign of overlordship. The year before the stipulated time for Mahomet to repair once more to Mecca was spent in consolidating his position by every means in his power. He was resolved that no weakness on his part should give the Kureisch the chance to refuse him again the entry into their city. His position was to be such that any question of ignoring the treaty would be made impossible, and by the time of Dzul Cada, 629, he had carried out his designs with that thoroughness of which only he in all Arabia seemed at that period capable.

Two thousand men gathered round him to participate in the important ceremony which was for them the visible sign of their kinship with the sacred city, and its ultimate religious absorption in their own all-conquering creed. They were clad in the dress of pilgrims, and carried with them only the sheathed sword of their compact for defence. But a body of men brought up the rear, themselves in armour, driving before them pack-camels, whereon rested arms and munitions of all kinds. Sixty camels were taken for sacrifice, and Mahomet, son of Maslama, with one hundred horse formed the vanguard, so as to prove a defence should the passions of the Kureisch overcome their discretion and nullify their plighted words. Abdallah, the impetuous, would fain have shouted some defiant words as the cavalcade neared the portals of the city, but Omar restrained him and Mahomet gave the command.

"Speak ye only these words, 'There is no God but God; it is He that hath upholden His servant. Alone hath He put to flight the hosts of the Confederates.'"

So any tumult was prevented and the truce carried out.

Then began one of the most wonderful episodes ever written upon the pages of history— nothing less than the peaceable emigration for three days of a whole city before the hosts of one who but a little time since had fled thence from the persecution of his fellows. All the Meccan armed population retired to the hills and left their city free for the completion of Mahomet's religious rites. With the sublimest faith in his integrity they left their city defenceless at his feet. Truly the Prophet's magnetism had won him many an adherent and secured him great triumphs in warfare, but never had his power shone with such lustre as at the time of his Fulfilled Pilgrimage. The city was left weaponless before his soldiery, and the dwellers within its walls were content to trust to the power of a written agreement, which in the hands of an unscrupulous man would be as effective as a reed against a whirlwind. Mahomet entered the city, and for three days pitched his tent of leather beneath the shadow of the Kaaba. He made the sevenfold circuit thereof and kissed the Black Stone. Thence he journeyed with all his followers to Safa and Marwa, where he performed the necessary rites, and at which latter place he sacrificed his victims, drawing them up in line between himself and the city. Then returning there he asked for and obtained the hand of Meimuna, sister-in-law of his uncle Abbas, a bold and characteristic stroke which did much to pave the way for the later conversion of his uncle and the final enrolment of the chief men of Mecca upon his side.

This was the last marriage he contracted, and it shows, as so many other alliances, his keen political foresight and the exercise of his favourite method of attempting to win over hostile states. He was still the political leader and schemer, though the ecstasy of religion, symbolised for him just now in the rites of the Lesser Pilgrimage, had caught him for the moment in its sweep. Public prayer was offered upon the third day from the Kaaba itself, and with that the Pilgrimage came to an end. Mahomet tried earnestly to win over and conciliate the Meccans during this meagre three days' sojourn, but his task was beyond the power even of his magnificent energy.

At the end of the third day the Meccans returned.

"Thy time is outrun: depart thou out of our city."

Mahomet answered: "What can it matter if ye allow me to celebrate my marriage here and make a feast as is the custom?"

But they replied with anger, "We need not thy feasts; depart thou hence."

And Mahomet was reluctantly forced to comply. He had been not without hope that the Kureisch would be won over to his cause in such great numbers that he might be suffered to remain as head of a converted Mecca, and he was loth to see such an unrivalled opportunity slip by without trying his utmost to gain some kind of permanent foothold in the city of his desires. But his faith weighed not so well with the Kureisch, and, having within himself the strength which knows when to desist from importunity, he quitted the city and retired to Sarif, eight miles away, where he rested together with his host of believers, now content and reverent towards the master who had made their dreams incarnate, their ideals tangible.

At Sarif Mahomet received what was perhaps the best fortune that had come to him outside his own powerful volition. Khalid, the skilful leader at Ohod and the greatest warrior the Kureisch possessed, together with Amru, poet and scholar as well as future warrior and conqueror of Egypt, were won over to the faith they had so obstinately opposed. They joined Mahomet at Sarif, and were forthwith appointed among the Companions, the equals of Ali, Othman and Omar. Following their adherence to the winning cause came the allegiance to Mahomet of Othman ibn Talha, custodian of the Kaaba. With these men of weight and influence ranged upon his side, the chief in war, the supreme in song, and the representative of Meccan ritualistic life, Mahomet had indeed justification for rejoicing. They were the first of the famous men and rulers in Mecca to range themselves with him, and they marked the turn of the tide, which came to its full flowing with the occupation of the sacred city and the conversion of Abu Sofian and Abbas.

Slowly, with pain and striving, Mahomet was overcoming the measureless opposition to things new. Six years of ceaseless effort, warfare and exhortation, compulsion and rewards were needed to secure for him the undisputed exercise of his religion in the place that was its sanctuary. Faith, backed by the strength and wealth of his armies, now gathered in the choicest of his opponents. The time was come when he was beginning to taste the wine of success. He had scarcely penetrated the borderland of that delectable garden, but the first meagre fruit thereof was sweet. It spurred him on to the perpetual renewal of alertness that he might keep what he had won and pursue his way to the innermost far-off enclosure, around the portal of which was written, as a mandate for all the world: "Bear witness, there is no God but God, and Mahomet is His Prophet."

The Fulfilled Pilgrimage, however, was but the preliminary to his master-stroke of policy strengthened by force of arms: months of hard fighting and diplomacy were needed before he could direct the blow that made his triumph possible. For the time he had simply made clear to Arabia that Mecca was his holy city, the queen of his would-be dominion, and by scrupulous performance of the old religious rites he had identified Islam both to his followers and to the Meccans themselves with the ancient fadeless traditions of their earlier faith, purified and made permanent by their homage to one God, "the Compassionate, the Merciful, the Mighty, the Wise."

CHAPTER XVIII

THE TRIUMPHAL ENTRY

"When the help of God and the Victory arrive,
And thou seest men entering the religion of God by troops,
Then utter the praise of thy Lord, implore His pardon, for He
loveth to turn in mercy."—*The Kuran.*

After the swordless triumph of Dzul Cada, 629, Mahomet rested in Medina for about nine months, while he sent out his leaders of expeditions into all parts of the peninsula wherever a rising was threatened, or where he saw the prospect of a conversion by force of arms. The Beni Suleim, whose more powerful allies, the Ghatafan, had given Mahomet much trouble in the past, were still recusant. Mahomet sent an expedition to essay their conversion early in the year, but the Suleim persisted in their enmity and received the Muslim envoys with a shower of arrows. They retired hastily, being insufficiently equipped to risk an attack, and came back to Medina. The Prophet, unabashed, now sent a detachment against the Beni Leith. The encampment was surprised, their camels plundered, their chattels seized, while they themselves were forced to flee in haste to the fastnesses of the desert. The Beni Murra, conquerors of Mahomet's expeditionary force at Fadak, received now at his hands their delayed but inevitable punishment. The Prophet found himself strong enough, and without any compunction he inflicted the severest chastisement upon them, more especially as an example to the neighbouring tribes of the retribution in store for all who dared to revolt against his newly-won but still precarious power.

Soon after an expedition of fifteen men was sent to Dzat Allah upon the borders of Syria. The men journeyed confidently to their far-off goal, but instead of finding, as they expected, a few chiefs at the head of ill-organised armies, they found arrayed against them an overwhelming force, well led and disciplined. They called upon them to embrace Islam with the fine courage of certain failure. The Bedouin hordes scoffed at the exhortation, and forthwith slew the whole company except one, who managed to escape to Medina with the tale. The catastrophe was a signal for a massed attack upon Mahomet's power from the whole of the border district, led by the feudatories of Heraclius, who were bent upon exterminating the upstart.

Hastily the Muslim army was mobilised, given into the leadership of Zeid, who with Jafar and Abdallah was commissioned to resist the infidels to the last and to continue their attack upon the foe until they were either slain or victorious. The army marched to Muta in September, 629, and while on the way heard with alarm of the massing of the foe, whose numbers daunted even their savage bravery.

At Muta a council of war was called at which Zeid and Abdallah were the principal speakers. After the peril of their position had been discussed and the reasons for retreat given, Abdallah rose from among his fellows, determined to rally their spirits. He pressed for an immediate advance, urging the invincibility of Allah, the power of their Prophet, and the glory of their cause. It was impossible for those warrior spirits not to respond to his enthusiasm, and the order was given. The Muslim marched to Beleea by the Dead Sea, but finding themselves in no good strategic position and hearing still further news as to the immensity of their opposition, they retired to Muta, where at the head of a narrow ravine they offered battle to the Roman auxiliaries, who far outweighed them in numbers and efficiency.

The Roman phalanx bore down upon them, and Zeid at the head of his troops urged them to resist with all their strength. He was cut down in the van as he led the opposing rush, and instantly Jafar, leaping from his horse, maimed it, as a symbol that he would fight to the death, and rushed forward on foot. The fight grew furious, and as the Muslim army saw itself slowly pressed back by the enemy its leader fell, covered with wounds. Abdallah seized the standard and tried to rally the Faithful, whose slow retreat was now breaking into a headlong flight. At his cry there was a brief rally, until in his turn he was cut down by the advancing foe. A citizen sprang to the standard and kept it aloft while he strove to stem the tide, but in vain. The Muslim ranks were broken and dispirited. They fell back quickly, and only the military genius of Khalid, in command of the rear, was able to save them from annihilation. He succeeded in covering their retreat by his swift and skilful moving, and enabled the remnant to return to Medina in safety.

Mahomet's grief at the loss of Jafar and Zeid was great. Jafar had only lately returned from Abyssinia, and was just at the beginning of his military career. He was the brother of Ali, and the martial spirit that had raised that warrior to eminence was only just now given opportunity to manifest itself. His loss was rightly felt by Mahomet to be a blow to the military as well as the intellectual prowess of Islam.

The Syrian feudatories, however, were not permitted to enjoy their triumph in peace. In October, 629, Amru, Mahomet's recent convert, was sent to chastise the offenders and exact tribute from them. He found the task was greater than he had imagined, and sent hurriedly to Medina for reinforcements. Abu Obeida was in command of the new army, and when he came up with Amru there was an angry discussion as to who should be leader. Abu Obeida had the precedent of experience and the asset of having been longer in Mahomet's service than Amru, but he was a mild man, fearful, and a laggard in dispute. Amru's impetuous determination overruled him, and he yielded to the compulsion of his more energetic rival, fearing to provoke disaster by prolonging the quarrel. The hostile Syrian tribes were rapidly dispersed with the increased forces at Amru's command, and he returned triumphant to Medina.

As a recompense for his yielding of the leadership to Amru, Abu Obeida was entrusted by Mahomet with the task of reducing the tribe of Joheina to submission. The expedition was wholly successful; the Joheina accepted the Prophet's yoke without opposition, and their lead was followed later in the year by the Beni Abs Murra and the Beni Dzobian, and finally the Beni Suleim, whose enmity in conjunction with the Beni Ghatafan had done much to prolong the siege of Medina.

The Prophet was exultant. The year's successes had surpassed his expectations, and the maturing of his deep-laid plans for the reduction of Mecca by pressure without bloodshed satisfied his ambitious and dominating soul. He was now master of Hedaz, overlord of Yemen and the Bedouin tribes of the interior as far as the dim Syrian border.

But with all his newly-found sovereignty there was one stronghold which he could neither conquer nor even impress. On the crowning achievement of subduing Mecca all his hopes were set, and there were no means that he did not employ to increase his power so that its continued resistance might ultimately become impossible. He strengthened his hold over the rest of Arabia; he won from Mecca as many allies as he could; he continually impressed upon both his followers and the surrounding tribes that the city was his natural home, the true abiding-place of his faith. Now, having prepared the way, he ventured to ensure the safety thereof by diplomacy and a skilful use of the demonstration of force. He was strong enough to compel an encounter with the Kureisch which should prove decisive.

In the attack upon the Khozaa, allies of the Prophet, the Beni Bekr, who gave their allegiance to the Kureisch, supplied Mahomet with the necessary *casus belli*. He declared upon the evidence of his friends that the Kureisch had helped the Beni Bekr in disguise and announced the swift enforcement of his vengeance. In alarm the Kureisch sent Abu Sofian to Medina to make their depositions as to the rights of the case and to beg for clemency. But their emissary met with no success. Mahomet felt himself powerful enough to flout him, and accordingly Abu Sofian was sent back to his native city discomfited.

There follows a tradition which has become obscured with the passing of time, and whose import we can only dimly investigate. Abu Sofian was returning somewhat uneasily to Mecca when he encountered the chief of the Khozaa, the outraged tribe. An interview of some length is reported, and it is supposed that the chief represented to the Meccan citizen the hopelessness of his resistance and the advantages in belonging to the party that was rapidly bringing all Arabia under its sway. Abu Sofian listened, and it may be that the chief's words induced him to consider seriously the possibility of ranging himself beneath the banner of the Prophet.

Meanwhile Mahomet had summoned all the matchless energy of which he was capable, and set on foot preparations for the overwhelming of Mecca. Every Believer was called to arms; equipment, horses, camels, stores were gathered in vast concourse upon the outskirts of Medina, awaiting only the command of the Prophet to go up against the scornful city whose humiliation was at hand. The order to march was given on January 1, 630, and soon the whole army was bearing down upon Mecca with that rapidity which continually characterised the Prophet's actions, and which was more than ever necessary now in face of the difficult task to be performed. In a week the Prophet, with Zeinab and Dram Salma as his companions, at the head of 10,000 men, the largest army ever seen in Medina, arrived within a stage of his goal. He encamped at Mar Azzahran and there rested his army from the long desert march, the toilsome and difficult route connecting the two long-sundered cities that had given feature to the origin and growth of Islam. While he was there he received what was perhaps the most important asset since the conversion of Khalid. Abbas, his uncle, still timorous and vacillating, but now impelled into a firmer courage by the powerful agency of Mahomet's recent triumphs, quitted Mecca with his following and joined his nephew, professing the creed of Islam, and enjoining it also upon those who accompanied him.

The conversion did not come as a surprise to Mahomet. He had been watching carefully by means of his spies the trend of events in Mecca, and he knew that the allegiance of Abbas was his whenever he should collect sufficient force to demonstrate his superiority. Abbas loved the winning cause. When Mahomet was obscure and persecuted he had befriended him as far as personal protection, but his was not the nature to venture upon a hazardous enterprise such as the Prophet's attempt to found a new religious community in another city. Now, however, that the undertaking had proved so completely victorious that it threatened to make of Mecca the weaker side, Abbas, with the solemnity which falls upon such people when self-interest points the same way as previous inclination, threw in his lot with Islam.

The Muslim rested that night at Mar Azzahran, kindling their camp-fires upon the crest of a hill whose summit could be seen from the holy city. The glare flamed red against the purple night sky, and by its ominous glow Abu Sofian ventured beyond the city's boundaries to reconnoitre. Before he could penetrate as far as the Muslim encampment he was met by Abbas, who took him straightway to Mahomet. When the morning came the Prophet sent for his rival and greeted him with contempt:

"Woe unto thee, Abu Sofian; seest thou not that there are no gods but God?"

But he answered with professions of his regard for Mahomet.

"Woe unto thee, Abu Sofian; believest thou not that I am the Prophet of God?"

"Thou art well appraised by us, and I see thy great goodness among the companions. As for what thou hast said I know not the wherefore of it."

Then Abbas, standing by Mahomet, besought him:

"Woe unto thee, Abu Sofian; become one of the Faithful and believe there is no god but God and that Mahomet is his Prophet before we sever thy head from the body!"

Under such strong compulsion, says tradition, Abu Sofian was converted and sent back to Mecca with promises of clemency. It is almost impossible not to believe that collusion between Abbas and Abu Sofian existed before this interview. Abbas had given the lead, for his prescience had divined the uselessness of resistance, and he foresaw greater glory as the upholder of Islam, the triumphing cause, than as the vain opposer of what he firmly believed to be an all-conquering power. Abu Sofian took somewhat longer to convince, and never really gave up his dream of resistance until he met Abbas on the fateful night and was shown the vastness of the Medinan army, their good organisation and their boundless enthusiasm. Thereat his hopes of victory became dust, and he bowed to the inevitable in the same manner as Abbas had done before him, though from different motives, one being actuated by the desire for favour and fame, the other only anxious to save his city from the horrors of a prolonged and ultimately unsuccessful siege.

Thereafter the army marched upon Mecca, and Mahomet completed his plans for a peaceful entry. Zobeir, one of his most trusted commanders, was to enter from the north, Khalid and the Bedouins from the southern or lower suburb, where possible resistance might be met, as it was the most populous and turbulent quarter. Abu Obeida, followed by Mahomet, took the nearest road, skirting Jebel Hind. It was an anxious time as the force divided and made its appointed way so as to come upon the city from three sides. Mahomet watched his armies from the rear in a kind of paralysis of thought, which overtakes men of action who have provided for every contingency and now can do nothing but wait. Khalid alone encountered opposition, but his skill and the force behind him soon drove the Meccans back within their narrow streets, and there separated them into small companies, robbing them of all concerted action, and rendering them an easy prey to his oncoming soldiery. Mahomet drew breath once more, and seeing all was well and that the other entries had been peacefully effected, directed his tent to be pitched to the north of the city.

It was, in fact, a bloodless revolution. Mahomet, the outcast, the despised, was now lord of the whole splendid city that stretched before his eyes. He had seen what few men are vouchsafed, the material fulfilment of his year-long dreams, and knew it was by his own tireless energy and overmastering faith that they had been wrought upon the soil of his native land.

His first act was to worship at the Kaaba, but before completing the whole ancestral rites he destroyed the idols that polluted the sanctuary. Then he commanded Bilal to summon the Faithful to prayer from the summit of the Kaaba, and when the concourse of Believers crowded to the precincts of that sacred place he knew that this occupation of Mecca would be written among the triumphant deeds of the world.

His victory was not stained by any relentless vengeance. Strength is always the harbinger of mercy. Only four people were put to death, according to tradition, two women-singers who had continued their insulting poems even after his occupation of the city, and two renegades from Islam. About ten or twelve were proscribed, but of these several were afterwards pardoned. Even Hind, the savage slayer of Hamza, submitted, and received her pardon at Mahomet's hands. An order was promulgated forbidding bloodshed, and the orderly settlement of Believers among the Meccan population embarked upon. Only one commander violated the peace. Khalid, sent to convert the Jadzima just outside the city, found them recalcitrant and took ruthless vengeance. He slew them most barbarously, and returned to Mecca expecting rewards. But Mahomet knew well the value of mercy, and he was not by nature vindictive towards the weak and inoffensive. He could punish without remorse those who opposed him and were his equals in strength, but towards inferior tribes he had the compassion of the strong. He could not censure Khalid as he was too valuable a general, but he was really grieved at the barbarity practised against the Jadzima. He effectually prevented any further cruelties, and on that very account rendered his authority secure and his rulership free from attempts to throw off its yoke within the vicinity of his newly-won power.

The populace was far too weak to resist the Muslim incursion. Its leaders, Abu Sofian and Abbas with their followings, had surrendered to the hostile faith; for the inhabitants there was nothing now between submission and death. The Believers were merciful, and they had nought to fear from their violence. They embraced the new faith in self-defence, and received the rulership of the Prophet very much as they had received the government of all the other chieftains before him.

One command, however, was to be rigidly obeyed, the command inseparable from the dominion of Islam. Idolatry was to be exterminated, the accursed idols torn down and annihilated. Parties of Muslim were sent out to the neighbouring districts to break these desecrators of Islam. The famous Al-Ozza and Manat, whose power Mahomet for a brief space had formerly acknowledged, were swept into forgetfulness at Nakhla, every image was destroyed that pictured the abominations, and the temples were cleansed of pollution.

Out of his spirit-fervour Mahomet's triumph had been achieved. In the dim beginnings of his faith, when nothing but its conception of the indivisible godhead had been accomplished, he had brought to its altars only the quenchless fire of his inspiration. He had not dreamed at first of political supremacy, only the rapture of belief and the imperious desire to convert had made his foundation of a city and then an overlordship inevitable. But circumstances having forced a temporal dominance upon him, he became concerned for the ultimate triumph of his earthly power. Thereupon his dreams took upon themselves the colouring of external ambitions. Conversion might only be achieved by conquest, therefore his first thoughts turned to its attainment. And as soon as he looked upon Arabia with the eyes of a potential despot he saw Mecca the centre of his ceremonial, his parent city, hostile and unsubdued. Certainly from the time of the Kureisch failure to capture Medina he had set his deliberate aims towards its humiliation. With diplomacy, with caution, by cruelty, cajolements, threatenings, and slaughter he had made his position sufficiently stable to attack her. Now she lay at his feet, acknowledging him her master—Mecca, the headstone of Arabia, the inviolate city whose traditions spoke of her kinship with the heroes and prophets of an earlier world.

Henceforward the command of Arabia was but a question of time. With Mecca subdued his anxiety for the fate of his creed was at an end. As far as the mastery of the surrounding country was concerned, all that was needed was vigilance and promptitude. These two qualities he possessed in fullest measure, and he had efficient soldiery, informed with a devoted enthusiasm, to supplement his diplomacy. He was still to encounter resistance, even defeat, but none that could endanger the final success of his cause within Arabia. Full of exaltation he settled the affairs of his now subject city, altered its usages to conform to his own, and conciliated its members by clemency and goodwill.

The conquest of Mecca marks a new period in the history of Islam, a period which places it perpetually among the ruling factors of the East, and removes it for ever from the condition of a diffident minor state struggling with equally powerful neighbours. Islam is now the master power in Arabia, mightier than the Kureisch, than the Bedouin tribes or any idolaters, soon to fare beyond the confines of its peninsula to impose its rigid code and resistless enthusiasm upon the peoples dwelling both to the east and west of its narrow cradle.

CHAPTER XIX

MAHOMET, VICTOR

> "Now hath God helped you in many battlefields and on the day of Honein, when ye prided yourselves on your numbers but it availed you nothing ... then ye turned your backs in flight. Then did God lend down his spirit of repose upon his Apostle and upon the Faithful, and he sent down the hosts which ye saw not and punished the Infidels."—*The Kuran.*

Mahomet's triumph at Mecca was not left long undisturbed. If the Kureisch had yielded in the face of his superior armies, the great tribe of the Hawazin were by no means minded to suffer his lordship, indeed they determined forthwith vigorously to oppose it. They were devoted to idol-worship, and leaven of Mahomet's teaching had not effected even remotely their age-long faith. They now saw themselves face to face not only with a religious revolution, but also with political absorption in the victorious sect if they did not make good their opposition to this overwhelming enemy in their midst.

They assembled at Autas, in the range of mountains north-east of Taif, and threatened to raid the sacred city itself. Mahomet was obliged to leave Mecca hurriedly after having only occupied the city for about three weeks. He left Muadh ibn Jabal to instruct the Meccans and secure their allegiance, and called off the whole of his army, together with 2000 of the more warlike spirits of his newly conquered territory. The force drew near the valley of Honein, where Mahomet fell in with the vanguard of the Hawazin. There the two armies, the rebels under Malik, the Muslim under the combined leadership of Khalid and Mahomet, joined battle. Khalid led the van and charged up the steep and narrow valley, hoping to overwhelm the Hawazin by his speed, but the enemy fell upon them from an ambuscade at the top of the hill and swept unexpectedly into the narrow, choked path. The Muslim, unprepared for the sudden onslaught, turned abruptly and made for flight. Instantly above the tumult rose the voice of their leader:

"Whither go ye? The Prophet of the Lord is here, return!"

Abbas lent his encouragement to the wavering files:

"Citizens of Medina! Ye men of the Pledge of the Tree of Fealty, return to your posts!"

In the narrow defile the battle surged in confluent waves, until Mahomet, seizing the moment when a little advantage was in his favour, pressed home the attack and, casting dust in the face of the enemy, cried:

"Ruin seize them! By the Lord of the Kaaba they yield! God hath cast fear into their hearts!"

The inspired words of their leader, whose vehement power all knew and reverenced, turned the day for the Muslim hosts. They charged up the valley and overwhelmed the troops at the rear of the Hawazin. The enemy's rout was complete. Their camp and families fell into the hands of the conqueror. Six thousand prisoners were removed to Jeirana, and the fugitive army pursued to Nakhla. Mahomet's losses were more severe than any which he had encountered for some time, but, undeterred and exultant, he marched to Taif, whose idolatrous citadel had become a refuge for the flying auxiliaries of the Hawazin.

Taif remained hostile and idolatrous. Ever since it had rejected his message with contumely, in the days when he was but a religious visionary inspired by a dream, it had refused negotiations and even recognition to the blasphemous Prophet.

Now Mahomet conceived that his day of vengeance had come. He invested the city, bringing his army close up to its walls, and hoping to reduce it speedily. But the walls of Taif were strong, its citadels like towers, its garrison well provisioned, its inmates determined to resist to the end. A shower of arrows from the walls wrought such destruction among his Muslim force that Mahomet was forced to withdraw out of range where the camp was pitched, two tents of red leather being erected for his favourite wives, Omm Salma and Zeineb. From the camp frequent assaults were made upon the town, which were carried out with the help of testudos, catapults, and the primitive besieging engines of the time.

But Taif remained inviolate, and each attack upon her walls made with massed troops in the hope of scaling her fortresses was received by heated balls flung from the battlements which set the scaling ladders on fire and brought destruction upon the helpless bodies of Mahomet's soldiery. But if he could not impress the city Mahomet wreaked his full vengeance upon its neighbourhood. The vineyards were cut down pitilessly, and the whole land of Taif laid desolate. Liberty was even offered to the slaves of the city who would desert to the invader. Nothing ruthless or guileful was spared by the Prophet to gain his ends, but with no avail. Taif held out until Mahomet grew weary, and finally raised the siege, which had considerably lessened in political importance, owing to the overtures of the Hawazin, who now wished to be reconciled with Mahomet, having perceived that their wisdom lay in peace with so powerful an adversary. They promised alliance with him and their prisoners were restored, but the booty taken from them was retained, after the old imperious custom, which demanded wealth from the conquered.

Mahomet forthwith distributed largesse among the lesser Arabs of the neighbourhood, an act of policy which called down the resentment of his adherents and caused the details of the law of almsgiving to be promulgated in the Kuran. The Muslim point of view was that having fought for the spoil they were entitled to receive a share of it, but their leader held that it must first be distributed in part to those needy Bedouin tribes who had flocked to his banner. The bounty had its desired effect. Malik, the Hawazin chieftain, moved either by his love of spoil or genuinely convinced of the truth of Islam, possibly by the influence of both these considerations, tendered his submission to Mahomet and became converted. February and March, 630, were occupied in distributing equitably the wealth that had fallen into his hands.

It was now the time of the Lesser Pilgrimage, and Mahomet returned to Mecca to perform it. Then, having fulfilled every ceremony and surrounded by his followers, he returned to Medina, still the capital of his formless principality and the keystone of his power.

Thereafter Mahomet rested in his own city, where he lived in potential kingship, receiving and sending out embassies, administering justice, instructing his adherents, but still keeping his army alert, his leaders well trained to quell the least disturbance or threatenings of revolt. The conquest of Mecca and the victory of Honein had rendered him secure from all except those abortive attacks that were instantly crushed by the marching of the force that was to subdue them.

The year 680-681 was spent in the receiving and sending out of embassies, alternating with the organising of small expeditions to chastise recusants, but to Mahomet himself there came besides the flower of an idyll, the frost of a grief.

Mary, the Coptic maid, young, lovely, and forlorn, the helpless barter of an Egyptian king, reached Medina in the first year of embassies and was reserved for the Prophet because of her beauty and her innocence. She had become long since a humble inmate of his harem, and would have ended her days in the same obscurity if potential motherhood had not come to her as an honour and a crowning. When Mahomet perceived that she was with child he had her removed from the company of his other wives, and built for her a "garden-house" in Upper Medina, where she lived until her child was born. Mahomet, returning from his campaigns, sought her in her retreat and gave her his companionship and his prayers.

In April of 630 she bore a son to her master, who could hardly believe that such a gift had been granted him. Never before had his arms held a man-child of his own begetting, and the honours lavished upon the slave-mother showed his boundless gratitude to Allah. A son meant much to him, for by that was ensured his hope for a continuance of power when his earthly sojourn was over. The child was named Ibrahim, and all the lawful ceremonies were scrupulously observed by his father. He sacrificed a kid upon the seventh day, and sought for the best and most fitting nurses for his new-born son. Mary received in full measure the smiles and favour of her master, and the Prophet's wives became jealous to fury, so that their former anger was revived—the anger that also had its roots in jealousy when Mahomet had first looked upon Mary with desiring eyes. Then they had gained their lord's displeasure as far as to cause a rebuke against them to be inscribed in the Kuran, but now their rage, though still smouldering, was useless against the triumph of that long-looked-for birth.

But Mahomet's joy was short-lived. Scarcely had three months passed when Ibrahim sickened even beneath the most devoted care. His father was inconsolable, and the little garden-house that had been the scene of so much rejoicing was now filled with sorrow. Ibrahim grew rapidly worse, until Mahomet perceived that there was no more hope. Then he became resigned, and having closed the child's eyes gave directions for its burial with all fitting ceremonial. Thereafter he knew that Allah had not ordained him an heir, and became reconciled to the vast decrees of fate. Mary, instrument of his hopes and despairs, passed into the oblivion of the despised and now useless slave. We never hear any more of her beyond that the Prophet treated her kindly and would not suffer her to be ill-used. She was the mere necessary means of the fulfilment of his intent. Having failed in her task she was no longer important, no longer even desired.

Meanwhile the tasks of administration had been increasing steadily. Mahomet was now strong enough to insist that none but Believers were to be admitted to the Kaaba and its ceremonies, and although all the idolatrous practices in Mecca were not removed until after Abu Bekr's pilgrimage, yet the power of polytheism was completely subdued, and before long was to be extirpated from the holy places.

The next matter to be taken in hand owes its origin to the extent of Mahomet's domains in the year 630. It was imperative that some sort of financial system should be adopted, so that the Prophet and the Believers might possess adequate means for keeping up the efficiency of the army, giving presents to embassies from foreign lands, rewarding worthy subjects, and all the numerous demands upon a chieftain's wealth. Deputies were therefore sent out to the various tribes now under his sway to gather from every subject tribe the price of their protection and championship by Mahomet.

In most cases the tax-gatherers were received as the inevitable result of submission, but there were occasional resistances organised by the bolder tribes, chief of whom was the Temim, who drove out Mahomet's envoy with contempt and ill-usage. Reprisals were immediately set on foot, the tribe was attacked and routed, many of its members being taken prisoner. These were subsequently liberated upon the tribe's guarantee of good faith. The Beni Mustalik also drove out the tax-gatherer, but afterwards repented and sent a deputation to Mahomet to explain the circumstance. They were pardoned and gave guarantees that they would dwell henceforth at peace with the Prophet. The summer saw a few minor expeditions to chastise resisters, chief of which was Ali's campaign against the Beni Tay. He was wholly successful, and brought back to Medina prisoners and booty.

The "second year of embassies" proved more gratifying than the first. Mahomet's power had increased sufficiently to awe the tribes of the interior into submission and to gain at least a hearing from lands beyond his immediate vicinity. Slowly and surely he was building up the fabric of his dominion. With a watchfulness and sense of organisation irresistible in its efficiency he made his presence known. The sword had gained him his dominion, the sword should preserve it with the help of his unfailing vigilance and diplomatic skill. As his power progressed it drew to itself not only the fighting material but the dreams and poetic aspirations of the wild, untutored races who found themselves beneath his yoke. Islam was before all an ideal, a real and material tradition, giving scope to the manifold qualities of courage, devotion, aspiration, and endeavour. Every tribe coming fully within its magnetism felt it to be the sum of his life, a religion which had not only an indivisible mighty God at its head, but a strong and resolute Prophet as its earthly leader. Around the central figure each saw the majesty of the Lord and also the headship of armies, the crown of power, and the sovereignty of wealth. They invested Mahomet with the royalty of romance, and the potency of his magnetism is realised in the story of the conversion of Ka'b the poet. He had for years voiced the feelings of contempt and anger against the Prophet, and had been the chief vehicle for the launching of defamatory songs. His conversion to the cause of Islam is momentous, because it deprived the idolaters of their chief means of vituperation and ensured the gradual dying down of the fire of abuse. Mahomet received Ka'b with the utmost honour, and threw over him his own mantle as a sign of his rejoicing at the acquisition of so potent a man. Ka'b thereupon composed the "Poem of the Mantle" in praise of his leader and lord, a poem which has rendered him famous and well-beloved throughout the whole Muslim world.

Now embassies came to Mahomet from all parts of Arabia. Instead of being the suppliant he became the dictator, for whose favour princes sued. Hadramaut and Yemen sent tokens of alliance and promises of conversion, even the far-off tribes upon the borders of Syria were not all equally hostile and were content to send deputations.

Nevertheless, it was from the North that his power was threatened. Secure as was his control over Central and Southern Arabia, the northern feudatories backed by Heraclius were still obdurate and even openly hostile. They were the one hope that Arabia possessed of throwing off the Prophet's yoke, which even now was threatening to press hardly upon their unrestrained natures. All the malcontents looked towards the North for deliverance, and made haste to rally, if possible, to the side of the Syrian border states. Towards the end of the year signs were not wanting of a concerted effort to overthrow his power on the part of all the northern tribes, who had as their ally a powerful emperor, and therefore might with reason expect to triumph over a usurper who had put his yoke upon their brethren of the southern interior, and was only deterred from attempting their complete reduction to the status of tributary states by the distance between his capital and themselves, added to the menace of the imperial legions.

CHAPTER XX

ICONOCLASM

"Oh Prophet, contend against the Infidels and the hypocrites, and be rigorous with them. Hell shall be their dwelling-place! Wretched the journey thither."—*The Kuran.*

The clouds upon the Syrian border gathered so rapidly that they threatened any moment to burst during the autumn of 680. When Mahomet heard that the feudatories were massed under the bidding of Heraclius at Hims, he realised there was no time to be lost. Eagerly he summoned his army, and expected from it the same enthusiasm for the campaign as he himself displayed.

But there was no generous response to his call. Syria was far away, the Believers could not be convinced of the importance of the attack. They were weary of the incessant warfare and it was, moreover, the season of the heats, when no man willingly embarked upon arduous tasks. The Companions rallied at once to the side of their leader, and many true Believers also supported their lord, but the Citizens and the Bedouins murmured against his exactions, and for the most part refused to accompany him.

Only Mahomet's indefatigable energy summoned together a sufficient army. But the Believers were generous, and gave not only themselves but their gold, and after some delay the expedition was organised.

Mahomet himself led the troop, leaving Abu Bekr in Medina to conduct the daily prayer and have charge of the religious life of the city, while to Molleima were given the administrative duties. The expedition reached the valley of Heja, where Mahomet called a halt, and there, about half-way from his goal, rested the greater part of two days. The next days saw him continually advancing over the scanty desert ways, urging on his soldiers with prayers and exhortations, so that they might not grow weary with the long heat and the silence. Finally he sighted Tebuk, where the rebel army was reported to be.

But by this time the border tribes had dispersed, frightened into inactivity by the strength of Mahomet's army, and incapacitated further by lack of definite leadership. There seemed no fighting to be done, but Mahomet was determined to make sure of his peaceful triumph. The main force stayed at Tebuk, while Khalid was despatched to Dumah, there to intimidate both Jews and Bedouins by the size of his force and their fighting prowess. The manoeuvre was entirely successful, and before long Mahomet had received the submission of the tribes dwelling along the shores of the Elanitic Gulf.

Meanwhile, he had recourse to diplomacy as well as the sword. He sent a letter to John, Christian prince of Eyla, and received from him a most favourable hearing. John accompanied the messenger back to the Prophet, where he accorded him meet reverence and regard as the leader of a mighty faith. Between the two princes a treaty was drawn up, the text of which is extant, and very probably authentic. It is characteristic of the whole series of treaties entered into at this time by Mahomet with the desert tribes, and as such is interesting enough to reproduce. These treaties are given at full length in Wakidi; they differ from each other by only small details, and that drawn up for John of Eyla may be taken as fairly representative. It is little more than a guarantee of safe conduct upon either side, and is noticeably free from any religious requirements or commissions:

"In the name of God, the Gracious, the Merciful. A compact of peace from God and from Mahomet, the Prophet and Apostle of God, granted unto Yuhanna, son of Rubah, and unto the people of Eyla. For them who remain at home and for those that travel by sea or by land, there is the guarantee of God and of Mahomet, the Apostle of God, and for all that are with them, whether of Syria or of Yeman, or of the Sea Coast. Whoso contraveneth this treaty, his wealth shall not save him—it shall be the fair prize of him that taketh it. Now it shall not be lawful to hinder the men of Eyla from any springs which they have been in the habit of frequenting, nor from any journey they desire to make, whether by sea or by land. The writing of Juheim and Sharrabil, by command of the Apostle of God."

When this scanty document had been completed John of Eyla betook himself again to his own country, leaving Mahomet free to enter into further compacts with the Jews of Mauna, Adzuh, and Jaaba. When these had been ratified and Mahomet had received tribute from the surrounding people, he set out again for Medina, having first made sure of Khalid's success in Dumah, and receiving the conversion of the chief of that tribe with much gladness.

Now, departing to Medina confident in his success, it was with no good will that he entered its walls. Many of his erstwhile followers, especially the tribes of Bedouins, had refused him their help upon this adventure, and, immediate danger being past, he returned to rend them in the fury of his eloquence. His success had given him the right to chastise; even the Ansar were not exempt from his wrath. Three who remained behind were proscribed, and compelled to fulfil fifty days of penance.

"Had there been a near advantage and a short journey, they would certainly have followed thee; but the way seemed long to them. Yet they will swear by God, 'Had we been able we had surely gone forth with you; they are self-destroyers! And God knoweth that they are surely liars!'"

Before he had entered the city his anger was further provoked by the Beni Ganim, who had erected a mosque, ostensibly out of piety, really to spite the Beni Amru ibn Auf and to make them jealous for their own mosque at Kuba, whose stones he had laid with his own hands. He fell upon the Ganim, "some who have built a mosque for mischief," and demolished the building. Then he drew attention to their perfidy in the Kuran, and took care that there should be no more mosques built in the spirit of rivalry and envy.

Very little time after his return to Medina, Abdallah, leader of the Disaffected, his opponent and critic for so many years, died suddenly. His death meant a great change in the position of his party. There was no strong man to succeed Abdallah, and they found themselves without leader or policy. They had for long been nominally allies of Mahomet, but had not scrupled under

Abdallah's leadership to question his authority by opposition and sometimes in open acts of war. Abdallah's death crushed for ever any attempts at revolt in Medina, and fused the Disaffected into the common stock of Believers.

Abdallah occupies rather a peculiar position in Mahomet's entourage; he was often the Prophet's opponent, sometimes his open defier, and yet Mahomet's dealings with him were uniformly gentle and forbearing. He may have had some personal regard for him. Abdallah was a stern and upright man, whose uncompromising nature would speedily win Mahomet's respect. Possibly the Prophet felt he might be too powerful an enemy, and determined to ignore his insurrections. He paid him that respect which his generosity of mind allowed him to offer towards any he knew and liked. The Mahomet whose ruthlessness towards his opponents fell like an awe upon all Arabia, could know and do homage to an enemy who had shown himself worthy of his steel. All things seemed to be working towards Mahomet's final prevailing. Now at last after many years the city of Medina was unfeignedly his, the Jews were extirpated, the Disaffected united under his banner.

Meanwhile, the city of Taif still held out in spite of Malik's incessant warfare against it. But its defences were steadily growing weaker, and at last the inhabitants knew they could no longer continue the hopeless struggle. The chief citizens sent an embassy to Mahomet, promising to destroy their idol within three years if the Prophet would release them from their harassment. But Mahomet refused unconditionally. The uprooting of idolatry was ever the price of his mercy. The message was sent back that instant demolition of the accursed thing must be made or the siege would continue. Then the people of Taif, hoping once more for clemency, asked to be released from the obligation of daily prayer. This request Mahomet also refused, but in deference to their ancestral worship, and no doubt in some pity for their plight, he allowed their idol to be destroyed by other hands than their own. Abu Sofian and Molleima were despatched with a covering force to destroy the great image Lat, which had stood for time immemorial in the centre of Taif and was the shrine for all the prayers and devotions of that fair and ancient city.

Taif was the last stronghold of the idolaters. When that had fallen beneath the sway of the Prophet and his remote, austerely majestic God-head, indivisible and personless, the doom of the old gods was at hand. They were dethroned from their high places at the bidding of a man; but they had not bowed their heads before his proclaimed message, but before the strength of his armies, the onward sweep of his ceaseless and victorious warfare. To Mahomet, indeed, Allah had never shown himself more gracious than at the fall of idolatrous Taif. He resolved thereupon that the crowning act of homage should be fulfilled. He would make a solemn journey to the holy city, and accomplish the Greater Pilgrimage with purified rites freed from the curse of the worship of many gods.

But when he came to the setting forth, and the sacred month of Dzul Higg was upon him, he found that many idolatrous practices still remained as part of the great ceremonial. He could not contaminate himself by undertaking the pilgrimage while these remained, but he could send Abu Bekr to ensure that none should remain after this year's cleansing. He was now strong enough to insist that the rooting out of idolatry was his chief policy, and to make the breaking up of the ancestral gods incumbent upon the whole country. Abu Bekr was commissioned to set forth upon his task with 300 men, and to spare neither himself nor them until the mission was accomplished and every idolatrous practice blotted out.

And now follows one of the most characteristic acts Mahomet ever performed, wherein obligation is made to bow to expediency and the bonds of treaties snap and break before the wind of the Prophet's will. Abu Bekr had started but one day's journey upon the Meccan road when Ali was sent after him with a document bearing the Prophet's seal. This he was to read to the Faithful, and receive their pledge that they would act upon its contents. Mahomet also published abroad a like proclamation in the city itself. The document drawn up and despatched with such haste was nothing less than a Release for the Prophet and his followers from all obligations to the Infidels after a term of four months.

"A Release by God and the Apostle in respect of the Heathen with whom ye have entered into treaty. Go to and fro in the earth securely in the four months to come. And know ye cannot hinder God, and that verily God will bring disgrace upon the Unbelievers. And an announcement from God and his Apostle unto the People on the day of Pilgrimage that God is discharged from (liability to) the Heathen and his Prophet likewise…. Fulfil unto these their engagements until the expiration of their terms; for God loveth the pious. And when the forbidden months are over then fight gainst the heathen, wheresoever ye find them, … but if they repent and establish Prayer and give the Tithes, leave them in peace…. O ye that believe, verily the Unbelievers are unclean. Wherefore let them not approach the Holy Temple after this year."

No one reading this writing, which bears upon it all the stamps of authenticity, can fail to see the motive behind its words. Its unscrupulousness has received in all good faith the sanction of the Most High. Mahomet knew that the time was ripe for an uncompromising insistence upon the acceptance of his faith. He was strong enough to compel. It was Allah who had strengthened his armies and given him dominion, therefore in Allah's name he repudiated his agreements with heathen peoples, and by virtue of his power he purposed to bestow upon his Lord a greater glory. An act wrought in such defiance of honour at the inspiration of God savours unquestionably of hypocrisy, but none who estimates aright the age and environment in which Mahomet dwelt can accuse him of anything more than a keenness of political cunning which led him to value accurately his own power and the waning reputation of idolatry.

The evil example he had set in this first Release extended with his conquests until it was accounted of universal application, and no Muslim considered himself dishonoured if he broke his pledge with any Unbeliever. From this time a more dogmatic and terrible note enters into his message. He openly asserts that idolatry is to be extirpated from Arabia by the sword, and that

Judaism and Christianity are to be reduced to subordinate positions. Judaism he had never forgiven for its rejection of him as Prophet and head of a federal state; Christianity he hated and despised, because to him in these later years monotheism had become a fanatic belief, and the whole conception of Christ's divinity was abhorrent to his worship of Allah. He was not strong enough to proclaim a destructive war against either faith, but he allowed them to exist in his dominions upon a precarious footing, always liable to abuse, attack, and profanation.

From the spring of 631 until the end of his life, Mahomet's campaigns consist in defensive and punitive expeditions. The realm of Arabia was virtually his, and the constant succession of embassies promising obedience and expressing homage continued until the end. But he was not allowed to enjoy his power in peace. The continuous series of small insurrections, speedily suppressed, which had accompanied his rise to power in later years, was by no means ended with his comparative security. But they never grew sufficiently in volume to threaten his dominion; they were wiped out at once by the alertness and political genius of his rule, until his death gave all the smaller chieftains fresh hope and became the signal for a desperate and almost successful attempt to throw off the shackles.

The first important conversion after his return from Taif was that of Jeyfar, King of Oman, followed closely by the districts of Mahra and Yemen, which localities had been hovering for some time between Islam and idolatry. The tribes of Najran were inclined to Christianity, and Mahomet was now anxious to gain them over to himself. The severity he had practised against a certain Christian church of Hanifa, however, weighed with them against any allegiance until he promised that theirs should be more favourably treated. A treaty was then made with these tribes by which each was to respect the religion of the other.

Mahomet remained in Medina throughout the year 631 and the beginning of 632, keeping his state like unto that of a king, surrounded by his Companions and Believers, receiving and sending forth embassies, receiving also tribute from those lands he had conquered, the beginning of that wealth which was to create the magnificence of Bagdad, the treasures of Cordova. The tribes of the Beni Asad, the Beni Kunda, and many from the territory of Hadramaut made their submission; tax-gatherers were also sent out to all the tributary peoples, and returned in safety with their toll. Almost it seemed as if peace had settled for good upon the land. The only threatenings came from the Beni Harith of the country bordering Najran, and the Beni Nakhla, with a few minor tribes near Yemen. Khalid was sent to call the Beni Harith to conversion at the point of the sword, and Ali subdued without effort the enfeebled resistance of the Beni Nakhla. Continual embassies poured into Medina. The country was quiet at last. After years of tumult Arabia had settled for the moment peaceably under the yoke of a religious enthusiast, who nevertheless possessed sufficient political and military genius to found his kingdom well and strongly.

Mahomet had attained his aims, and whether he could keep what he had now rested with himself alone. After this period of calm there is a diminution in his energy and fiery zeal. The effort of that continual warfare had kept him in perpetual fever of action; when its strain was removed he felt the weight of his kingdom and the religion he had so fearlessly reared. Until the end of his life he kept his hold upon his subjects, and every branch of justice, law, administration, and military policy felt his detailed guiding, but with the attainment of peace for Arabia under his sway, his aggressive strivings vanished. Virtually he had accomplished his destiny, and with the keen prescience of those who have lived and worked for one object, he knew that the outermost stronghold of those which Islam was destined to subdue had yielded to his passionate insistence. His successors would carry his work to higher attainments, but his personal part was done, and it was with a sense of finality that almost brought peace to his perpetually striving nature that he prepared for his last witness to the glory and unity of Allah, the performance of the Greater and Farewell Pilgrimage.

CHAPTER XXI

LAST RITES

> "This day have I perfected your religion for you, and have filled up the measure of my favours upon you; and it is my pleasure that Islam be your religion."—*The Kuran.*

A year had passed since Abu Bekr's purgatory Pilgrimage, and now the sacred month drew near once more and found Mahomet secure in his adopted city, the acknowledged spiritual and political leader among the Arabian tribes. Not since his exile had the Prophet performed in their entirety the rites of the Greater Pilgrimage. Now he felt that his achievements would receive upon them the seal of Allah and become attested in the eyes of the world if he should undertake a complete and purified Pilgrimage in company with the host of his followers. The Pilgrimage was proclaimed abroad in Islam, and every Believer who could by any means accomplish it assumed the Pilgrim's garb, until the army of the devout numbered about 40,000 men. All the Prophet's wives accompanied him, and every Believer of any standing in the newly formed state was his close attendant. It was felt, indeed, that this was to be the Pilgrimage that was to ordain and sanction the rite for all time. In the deepest spirit of religion and devotion it was undertaken and completed. Islam was now to show to the world the measure of its strength, and to succeeding generations the sum of its being and the insistence of its call.

With the host travelled also a hundred camels, destined as a sacrifice upon the triumphant day when the ceremonies should be accomplished. By easy stages the Pilgrims journeyed through the desert. There was no hurry, for there was no fear of attack. The whole company was unarmed, save for the defensive sword allowed to each man. Over the desert they moved like locusts, overwhelming the country, and the tune of their march spread far around. In ten days the pilgrim army, in the gladness of self-confidence and power, arrived at Sarif, a short day's march from their goal. There Mahomet rested before he embarked upon the final journey.

Mecca lay before him, awaiting his coming, her animosities silenced, her populace acquiescent, her temples freed from the curse of idolatry. His mind was uplifted into a fervour of praise. He seemed in truth about to enter upon his triumph, to celebrate in very flesh the ceremonies he had reverenced, to celebrate them in his own peculiar manner, freed of what was to him their bane and degradation. Something of the foreknowledge of the approaching cessation of activity flashed across him as he mounted Al-Caswa and prepared to make the entry of the city.

He came upon the upper suburbs by the same route as he had entered Mecca two years before, and proceeded to the Kaaba. There he performed the circuits of the sacred place and the preliminary rites of the Greater Pilgrimage. Then he returned to the valley outside the city where his tent was pitched, and tarried there the night. And now Ali, the mighty in arms, reached the city from an admonitory expedition and demanded the privilege of performing the Pilgrimage. Mahomet replied that like most other Believers he might perform the rites of the Lesser Pilgrimage, but that the Greater was barred to him because he had no victims. But Ali refused to forego his privilege, and at last Mahomet, urged by his love for him and his fear of creating any disturbance at such a time, felt it wiser to yield. He gave Ali the half of his own victims, and their friendship and Ali's devotion to his master were idealised and made sweeter for the gift.

Now the rites of the Greater Pilgrimage properly began. Mahomet preached to the people from the Kaaba on the morning of the next day, and when his words had roused the intense religious spirit of those listening masses he set out for Mina, accompanied by Bilal, followed by every Believer, and prepared to spend the night in the sacred valley. When morning dawned he made his way to Arafat, where he climbed the hill in the midst of the low-lying desolate ground. Standing at the summit of the hill, surrounded by the hosts of his followers, revealed to their eyes in all the splendour and dignity of his familiarity and personally wrested authority, he recited some of the verses of the Kuran dealing with the fit and proper celebration of the Pilgrimage. He expounded then the manner in which that rite was to be performed for all time. So long as there remains one Muslim upon earth his Pilgrimage will be carried out along the traditions laid down for him at this beneficent moment.

Now, having ordered all matters, Mahomet raised his hands to Heaven and called Allah to witness that he had completed his task:

"This day have I perfected your religion for you."

The supreme moment came and fled, and the Prophet descended once more into the plain and journeyed again to the valley of Mecca, where, according to immemorial tradition, he cast stones, or rather small pebbles, at the rock of the Devil's Corner, symbolic of the defeat of the powers of darkness by puny and assailed mankind. Thereafter he slew his victims in thankful and devout spirit, and the Greater Pilgrimage was completed. In token he shaved his head, pared his nails, and removed the pilgrim's robe; then, coming before the people, he exhorted them further, enjoining upon them the strict observance of daily prayers, the fast of Ramadan, the rites of Pilgrimage, and all the essential ceremonial of the Muslim faith. He abolished also with one short verse of the Kuran the intercalary year, which had been in use among the Faithful during the whole of his Medinan rule. The Believers were now subject to the fluctuation of their months, so that their years follow a perpetually changing cycle, bearing no relation to the solar seasons.

When the exhortation was ended Mahomet departed to Mecca, and there he encircled the Kaaba and entered its portals for prayer. But of this last act he repented later, inasmuch as it would not be possible hereafter for every Muslim to do so, and he had desired to perform in all particulars the exact ceremonies incumbent upon the Faithful for all the future years. He now made an ending of all his observances, and with every rite fulfilled, at the head of his vast concourse, summoned by his tireless will and held together by his overmastering zeal, the Prophet returned to his governmental city, ready to take up anew the reins of his temporal ruling, with the sense of fine things fittingly achieved, a great purpose accomplished, which rendered him as much at peace as his fiery temperament and the flame of his activity could compass.

Fulfilment had come with the performance of the Greater Pilgrimage, but still his state demanded his personal government. Death alone could still his ardent pulses and bring about his relinquishment of command over the kingdom that was his—death that was even now winging his silent way nearer, and whose shadow had almost touched the fount of the Prophet's earthly life.

In such manner the Greater Pilgrimage was fulfilled, and the burden of its accomplishing is the Muslim reverence for ceremony. The ritual in all its forgotten superstition and immemorial tradition appealed most potently to the emotions of every Believer, all the more so because it had not been imposed upon him as a new and untried ceremony by a religious reformer, but came to him with all its hallowed sanctity fresh upon it, to be bound up inseparably with his religious life by its purification under the Prophet's guidance.

Its use by the founder of Islam bears witness at once to his knowledge of the earlier faith and traditions and his reverence for them, as well as his keen insight, which placed the rite of pilgrimage in the forefront of his religious system. He knew the value of ritual and the force of age-long association. The Farewell Pilgrimage is the last great public act he performed. He felt that it strengthened Islam's connection with the beliefs and ceremonies of his ancestors, legendarily free from idolatry under the governance of Abraham and Ishmael. He realised, too, that it rounded off the ceremonial side of his faith, giving his followers an example and a material union with himself and his God. It was the knowledge that this union would always be a living fact to his descendants, so long as the sacred ceremony was performed, that caused him to assert its necessity and to place it among the few unalterable injunctions to all the Faithful.

Meanwhile a phenomenon had arisen inseparable from the activities of great men. Wherever there are strong souls, from whose spirit flows any inspiring energy, there will always be found their imitators, when the battle has been won. Whether hypocrites, or genuinely led by a sheep-like instinct into the same path as their models, they follow the steps of their forerunners, and usually achieve some slight fame before the dark closes around them.

Early in the year Badzan, Governor of Marab, Nazran, and Hamadan, died. His territory was seized by Mahomet, in defiance of the claims of his son Shehr, and divided among different governors. His success in the temporal world, and especially this peaceful annexation of land, wrought so vividly upon the imaginations of his countrymen that three false Prophets arose and three separate bands of devoted fanatics appeared to uphold them. Of these three men the most effective was Tuleiha of the Beri Asad, who gathered together an army and was only repelled and crushed by Khalid himself. But Tuleiha still persisted in spite of defeat, and was content to bide his time until, under Abu Bekr, his faction rose again to importance and constituted a serious disturbance to the rule of the first Caliph.

Moseilama, of whom not so much is known, also attempted to usurp the Prophet's power at the close of his life. Mahomet demanded his submission; Moseilama refused, but before adequate punishment could be meted out the Prophet was stricken down with illness, so that the task of chastisement devolved upon Abu Bekr. Aswad, "the veiled Prophet of Yemen," might have proved the most formidable of the three, had not rashness of conduct and lack of governance caused his undoing. He cast off the Muslim yoke while the Prophet was still alive, and proclaimed himself the magician prince who would liberate his followers from the tyrant's yoke. Najran rose in his favour, and he marched confidently upon Sana, the great capital city of Yemen, slew the puppet king Shehr and took command of the surrounding country. Mahomet purposed to send a force against him, but even while his army was massing for the march he heard that the Veiled Prophet was assassinated. The sudden success had proved his ruin. Aswad only needed the touch of power to call out his latent tyranny, cruelty, and stupidity. He treated the people harshly, and they could not retaliate effectually; but he forgot, being of unreflecting mould, the imperative necessity of conciliating the chiefs of his armed forces. He offended his leaders of armies, and the end came swiftly. The leaders deserted to Mahomet, and treacherously murdered him when he had counted their submission was beyond question. The three impostors were not powerful enough to disturb seriously the steady flow of Mahomet's organising and administrative activities, but they are indicative of the thin crust that divided his rule from anarchy, a crust even now cracking under the weight of the burdens imposed upon it, needing the constant cement of armed expeditions to keep it from crumbling beyond Mahomet's own remedying.

April passed quietly enough at Medina, but with May came the news of fresh disturbances upon the Syrian border. They were not serious, but the pretext was sufficient. Muta was as yet unavenged, and Mahomet was glad to be able to send a force again to the troublesome frontier. Osama, son of Zeid, slain in that disastrous battle, was chosen for leader of this expedition in spite of his youth, which aroused the quick anger of some of the Muslim warriors. But Mahomet maintained his choice. He was given the battle banner by the Prophet himself, and the expedition sallied forth to Jorf, where it was delayed and finally hastily recalled by news of a grave and most disturbing nature.

Even as he blessed the Syrian expedition and sent it on its road, Mahomet was in no fit state of health for public duties. After a little while, however, his will triumphed over his flesh, and he thrust back the weakness. But his physical nature had already been strained to breaking point under the stress of his life. He had perforce to bow to the dictates of his body. He gave up attempting to throw off the fever, and retired to Ayesha's house, attributing the seizure to the effects of the poison at Kheibar, and convinced that his end was at hand.

In the house of his favourite wife he remained during the few remaining days of his life. He lingered for about a week before his indomitable soul gave way before the assaults of death, and all the time he continued to attend to public affairs and to take his accustomed part in them as long as possible. About the third day of his illness he heard the people still murmuring over the appointment of Osama upon the Syrian expedition. Rising from his couch he went out to speak to them, and commanded them to cease from such empty discontent, reminding them that he was their Prophet and master, and that they might safely rely upon him.

The exertion of moving proved too much for his strength. He was now indeed a broken man, and this activity was but the last conquest of mind over his ever-growing weakness of body. He returned exhausted to Ayesha's room, and, knowing that his mission was over, commanded Abu Bekr to lead the public prayers. By this act he virtually nominated Abu Bekr his successor; for the privilege of leading the prayers belonged exclusively to himself, and his designation of the office was as plain a proof as there could be that he considered the mantle of authority to have descended upon his friend and counsellor, who had been to him so unfailing a resource in defeat and triumph through all the tumultuous years.

From this time the Prophet grew steadily worse. His physical break-up was complete. He had used every particle of his enormous energy in the fulfilment of his work; now that activity had ceased there were no reserves left.

He became delirious, and finally weak to the point of utter exhaustion. Many are the traditions concerning his dying words, chiefly exhortations for the preservation of the faith he had so laboriously brought to life. He is said to have cursed both Jews and Christians in his paroxysms of fever, but in his lucid moments he seems to have been filled with love for his disciples, and fears for the future of his religion and temporal state.

He lingered thus for two more days—days which gathered round him the deep spiritual fervour, the human love and affection of every Believer, so that the records are interpenetrated with the grief and tenderness of a people's sorrow. On the third day he rallied sufficiently to come to morning prayer, where he took a seat by Abu Bekr in token of his dedication of the headship of Islam to him alone. The Believers' joy at the sight of their Prophet showed itself in their thronging thanksgivings and in their escort of their chief back to his place of rest. It seemed that his illness was but slight, and that before long he would appear among them once more in all the fullness of his strength. But the exertion sapped his little remaining vitality, and he could scarcely reach Ayesha's room again. There a few hours afterwards, after a period of semi-consciousness, he died in her arms while it was yet only a little after mid-day.

The forlorn Ayesha was almost too terrified to impart the dreadful news. Abu Bekr was summoned instantly, and came with awe and horror into the mosque. Omar, Mahomet's beloved warrior-friend, refused to believe that his leader was really dead, and even rushed to announce his belief to the people. But Abu Bekr visited the place of death and assured himself by the still cold form of the Prophet that he was indeed dead. He went out with despair in his countenance, and convinced the Faithful that the soul of their leader had passed. There fell upon Islam the hush of an intolerable knowledge, and in the first blankness of realisation they were dumb and passive.

When the army at Jorf was apprised of the news, it broke up at once and returned to Medina. With the withdrawal of the guiding hand their battle enthusiasm became as nought, and they could only join the waiting ranks of the Citizens—a crowd that would now be driven whither its masters saw fit.

The Faithful assembled round the mosque to question the future of themselves and their rulers. Abu Bekr addressed them at once, and it was soon evident that he had them well in hand. He was supported by Omar and the chief leaders, except Ali, who maintained a jealous attitude, chiefly due to the feelings of envy aroused in the mind of Fatima, his wife, at the sight of Ayesha's privileges. At last, when Abu Bekr had told the circumstances of the Prophet's death, tenderly and with that loving reverence which characterised him, the Faithful were attuned to the acceptance of this man as their Prophet's successor. The chief men, followed by the rank and file, swore fealty to him, and covenanted to maintain intact and precious the Faith bequeathed them by their leader, who had been also their guide and fellow-worshipper of Allah.

There remained only the last dignity of burial. The Prophet's body was washed and prepared for the grave. Around it was wrapped white linen and an outer covering of striped Yemen stuff.

Abu Bekr and Omar performed these simple services for their Prophet, and then a grave was dug for him in Ayesha's house, and a partition made between the grave and the antechamber. It was dug vaulted fashion, and the body deposited there upon the evening of the day of death. The people were permitted to visit it, and after the long procession had looked their last upon their Prophet, Abu Bekr and Omar delivered speeches to the assembled multitude, urging them to remain faithful to their religion, and to hold before them continually the example of the Prophet, who even now was received into the Paradise he had described so ardently and loved with such enshrining desire.

Thus the Prophet of Islam, religious and political leader, director of armies, lover of women, austere, devout, passionate, cunning, lay as he would have wished in the simplicity of that communal life, in the midst of his followers, near the sacred temple of his own devising. He had lived close to his disciples, had appeared to them a man among men, indued only with the divine authority of his religious enthusiasm; now he rested among them as one of themselves, and none but felt the inspiration of his energy inform their activities after him, though the manifestation thereof confined itself to the violence necessary to maintain the Prophet's domain secure from its earthly enemies.

Mahomet, indeed, in his mortal likeness rested in the quiet of Ayesha's chamber, but his spirit still led his followers to prayer and conquest, still stood at the head of his armies, urging to victory and plunder, so that they might find in the flaunting banners of Islam the fulfilment of their lusts and aspirations, their worldly triumphs and the glories of their heavenly vision.

CHAPTER XXII

THE GENESIS OF ISLAM

"The Jews say, 'Ezra is a son of God,' and the Christians say, 'The Messiah is a son of God' … they resemble the saying of the Infidels of old…. They take their teachers and their monks and the Messiah, son of Mary, for Lords beside God, though bidden to worship one God only. There is no God but He! Far what from his glory be what they associate with Him."—*The Kuran*.

The Prophet of Arabia had scarcely been committed to the keeping of earth, when on all sides rebellion against his rule arose. The unity that he had laboured so long to create was still in embryo, but the seed of it was living, and developed rapidly to its full fruition. In the political sphere his achievement is not limited to the immediate security of his dominion. He had inculcated, mainly by the forcible logic of the sword, the idea of union and discipline, and had restored in mightier degree the fallen greatness of his land. Traditions of Arabian prosperity during the time when it was the trade route from Persia and the East to Petraea, Palestine, and even Asia Minor lingered in the native mind. The caravan routes from Southern Arabia, famous in Biblical story, had made the importance of such cities as Mecca and Sana, but with the maritime enterprise of Rome their well-being declined, and the consequent distress in Yemen induced its tribes to emigrate northwards to Mecca, to Syria, and the Central Desert. Southern Arabia never recovered from the blow to its trade, and in the sixth century Yemen became merely a dependency of Persia. Central Arabia was an unknown country, inhabited by marauding tribes in a constant state of political flux; while Hira, the kingdom to the east of the desert on the banks of the Euphrates, had become a satrapy of Persia early in the century in which Mahomet lived, and Heraclius by frequent inroads had reduced the kingdom of Palmyra to impotence. Arabia was ripe for the rise of a strong political leader; for it was flanked by no powerful kingdom, and within itself there was no organisation and no reliable political influence.

The material was there, but it needed the shaping of a master-hand at the instigation of unflagging zeal if it was to be wrought into order and strength. Tireless energy and unceasing belief in his own power could alone accomplish the task, and these Mahomet possessed in abundance. Before his death he had secured the subjection of Yemen and Hadramaut, had penetrated far into the Syrian borderland, and had made his rule felt among the nomad tribes of the interior as far as the confines of Persia. With his rise to power the national feeling of Arabia was born, and under his successors developed by the enticements of plunder and glory until it soared beyond mere nationality and dreamt of world-conquest, by which presumption its ruin was wrought. Mahomet was the instigator of all this absorbing activity, although he never calculated the extent of his political impulse. In superseding the already effete tribal ideals he was to himself only spreading the faith of his inspiration. All governmental conceptions die slowly, and the tribal life of Arabia was far from extinguished at the end of his mission. But its vitality was gone, and the focus of Arabia's obedience had shifted from the clan to the Prophet as military overlord.

It is pre-eminently in the domain of political actions that Mahomet's personality is revealed. The living fibres of his unique character pulse through all his dealings with his fellow-leaders and opponents. Before all things he possessed the capacity of inspiring both love and fear. Ali, Abu Bekr, Hamza, Omar, Zeid, every one of his followers, felt the force of his affection continually upon them, and were bound to him by ties that neither misfortune nor any unworthy act of his could break. And their devotion was called upon to suffer many tests. Mahomet was self-willed and ruthless, subordinating the means to the end without any misgivings. In his remorseless dealings with the Jews, in his calm repudiation of obligations with the heathen as soon as he felt himself strong enough, he shows affinities to the most conscienceless statesman that ever graced European diplomacy.

His method of conquest and government combines watchfulness and strength. No help was scorned by this builder of power. What he could not achieve by force he attempted to gain by cunning. He had a large faith in the power of argument backed by force, and his winning over of Abbas and Abu Sofian chiefly by the aid of these two factors, combined with their personal ambition, is only the supreme instance of his master-strokes of policy. He knew how to play upon the baser passions of men, and especially was he mindful of the lure of gold. His first forays against the Kureisch were set before the eyes of his disciples as much in the light of plundering expeditions as religious wars against an infidel and oppressive nation.

He is at once the outcome of circumstances, and independent of them. He gave coherence to all the unformulated desires for a fuller scope of military and mercantile power stirring at the fount of Arabia's life, and at the same time he founded his dominion in a unique and absolutely personal manner. Within his sphere of governance his will was supreme and unassailable.

If these mutable tribal entities were to be united at all, despotism was the only possible form of command. As his polity demanded authority vested in one person only, so his conception of God is that of an absolute monarch, resistance to whom is annihilation.

Out of this idea the doctrine of fatalism was evolved. It was necessary during the first terrible years of uncertainty in Islam, in order to produce among Mahomet's followers a recklessness in battle, and in the varying fortunes of their life at Medina, born of the knowledge that their fate was irrevocably decided. They fought for the true God against the idolaters; this true God held their destinies in his hand; nothing could be altered. The result was that the Muslim fought with superhuman daring, and faced overwhelming forces undaunted. But the time came when Islam had no longer any need to fight, and the doctrine of fatalism still lived. It sank into mental and physical inactivity, and of that inactivity, induced by the knowledge that their energies were unavailing, pessimism was bred. Despotism and fatality are perhaps the purely personal ideas that Mahomet gave to his political state, the latter encroaching, however, as most of his secular principles, upon the realm of philosophy. Indeed, his political rule is inseparable from his religion, and as a religious leader he is more justly appraised.

In the sphere of religion the raw material was to his hand. At the inception of his mission Mecca and Central Arabia, though confirmed in idolatry, still mingled with their rites some distorted Jewish traditions and ceremonies, while Yemen had embraced the Christian faith for a short time as a dependency of Abyssinia, but had relapsed into idolatry with the interference of Persia. Both the border kingdoms to the north, Palmyra and Hira, were Christian, and in the time of their prosperity had influenced Arabia in the direction of Christianity. The Christian Scriptures were known and respected, but these impulses were feeble and spasmodic, so that the bulk of Arabia remained fixed in its ancient idolatry.

By far the more enduring influence was that of Judaism. Many Jewish tribes were settled in Arabia, and the ancient traditions of the Jewish race, the great figures of Abraham, Lot, and Noah were set vividly before the eyes of the Arabs. There was every indication that a religious teacher might use the existing elements of Judaism and Christianity to produce a monotheistic faith, partaking of their nature, and for a time Mahomet endeavoured to bring both forms within the scope of his mission. But compromise, whether with idolaters or Jews, was found to be impossible, and here religious and political ideals are inextricably blended. If Mahomet had acquiesced in the Jewish religion, had submitted to the sovereignty of Jerusalem as the Holy Place, he would have found it impossible to have established his supremacy in Medina, and the religion of Islam as he conceived it would have been overriden by the older and more hallowed faith of the Jews. He saw the danger, and his dominant spirit could not allow the existence of an equal or superior power to his own. With that fiery daring and supreme belief in his destiny which characterised him in later life, he cast away all pretensions to friendliness either with the Jews or the Christians, and steered his followers triumphantly through the perils that beset every adherent to an idea.

But in compelling acceptance of his central thesis of the unity of the Godhead, he showed signal wisdom and knowledge of men. He was himself by no means impervious to the value of tradition, and never conceived his faith as having no historical basis in the religious legends of his birthplace. That the Muslim belief possesses institutions such as the reverence for the Kaaba, the rite of Pilgrimage, the acceptance of Mecca as its sacred city, is due to its founder's love of his native place, and the ceremonial of which his own creed was really the inseparable outcome.

Besides his recognition of the need of ritual, he was fully aware of the repugnance of most men to the wholly new. Whenever possible he emphasized his connection with the ancient ceremonies of Mecca in their purer form, and as soon as his power was sufficient, he enforced the recognition of his claims upon the city itself.

His achievement as religious reformer rests largely upon the state of preparation in which he found his medium, but it owes its efficiency to one force alone. Mahomet was possessed of one central idea, the indivisibility of God, and it was sufficient to uphold him against all calamities. The Kuran sounds the note of insistence which rings the clarion call of his message. With eloquence of mind and soul, with a repetition that is wearisome to the outsider, he forces that dominant truth into the hearts of his hearers. It cannot escape them, for he will not cease to remind them of their doom if they do not obey. What he set out to do for the religious life of Arabia he accomplished, chiefly because he concentrated the whole of his demands into one formula, "There is no God but God"; then when success had shown him the measure of his ascendancy, "There is no God but God, and Mahomet is His prophet."

At the end of his life idolatry was uprooted from his native country. The tribes might rebel against the heaviness of his political yoke, and were often held to him by the slenderest of diplomatic threads, but their monotheistic beliefs remained intact once Islam had gained the ascendancy over them. At the end of the Farewell Pilgrimage, he realised with one grand uplifting of his soul in thanksgiving that he had indeed caught up the errant attempts of Arabia to remodel its unsatisfying faith, and had made of them a triumphant reality, in which the conception of Allah's unity was the essential belief.

Besides his religious and political attainments, he gave to Arabia as a whole its first written social and moral code. Here the estimate of his accomplishment is difficult to render, bemuse comparison with the existing state is almost impossible. Extensively in the Kuran, but to a greater degree in the mass of his traditional sayings, crystallised into a standard edition by Al-Bokhari, when due allowance has been made for the additions and exaggerations of his followers, the chief characteristic is the casual nature of his laws.

All his dictates as to the control of marriage, the sale and tenure of land, commerce, plunder, as well as health and dietary are the result of definite cases coming within his adjudication. Such an idea as the deliberate compilation of a code never occurred to him, and there is no evidence that he ever referred to his former decisions in similar cases, so that possibilities of contradiction and evasion are limitless. Out of this jumble of inconsistencies Muslim law and practice has grown. He was enabled to impose his commands upon the conquered peoples by means of his military organisation, so that it was not long before Arabia was ruled in rough fashion by his social and moral precepts enforced by the sword. His wives offend him, and he forthwith sets down the duties and position of women in his temporal state. He desires the wife of his friend, and the result is a Kuranic decree sanctioning the taking of a woman under those conditions. He is jealous of his younger and more comely associates, and thereupon ordains the perpetual seclusion of women. He is annoyed at the untimely visits to his house of assembly, and so he commands that no Believer shall enter another's apartment uninvited. It is inconvenient to relinquish the watch night or day during the period of siege in Medina, therefore he institutes a system whereby half the army is to pray while the other half remains at its post. Instances may be multiplied without ceasing of this building up of a whole social code upon the most casual foundations. But unheeding as was its genesis, it was in the main effective for those times, and in any case it substituted definite laws for the measureless wastes of tradition and custom.

It is probable that Mahomet relied a great deal upon existing usages. He was too wise to disturb them unnecessarily. His was a nature of extremes combined with a wisdom that came as a revelation to his followers. Where he hates it is with a hurricane of wrath and destruction, where he loves it is with the same impetuous tenacity. His denunciations of the infidels, of his enemies among the Kureisch, of the laggards within his own city, of the defamers of holy things, of drunkards, of the unclean, of those who even copy the features of their kindred or picture their idea of God, are written in the most violent words, whose fury seems to smite upon the ear with the rushing of flame.

And so the prevailing stamp upon Muslim institutions is fanaticism and intolerance. As the Prophet drew up hard-and-fast rules, so his followers insisted upon their remorseless continuance. Mahomet found himself compelled to issue ordinances, often hurried and unreflecting, to meet immediate needs, to settle disputes whose prolongation would have meant his ruin. He possessed the qualities of poet, seer, and religious mystic, but these in his later life were overshadowed by the characteristics of lawgiver, soldier, and statesman demanded by his position as head of a body of men. But neither his mysticism nor his poetic feeling entirely desert him. They flash out at rare moments in the later suras of the Kuran, and are apparent in his actions and the traditional accounts of his sayings, while his creed remained steadfast and unassailable with a strength that neither defeat nor disaffection could shake. With all the incompleteness and often contradiction of his administration, he nevertheless was able to satisfy his followers as to its efficacy mainly by his exhaustless belief in himself and his work.

In military development his contribution was unique. He gathered together all the war-loving propensities of the Faithful, and wove them into a solidarity of aim. His personal courage was not great, but his strategy and above all his invincible confidence, which refused to admit defeat, were beyond question. Every leader he sent upon plundering or admonitory expeditions bore witness to his efficiency and his zeal. He subjected the Muslim to a discipline that brought out their best qualities of tenacity and daring. He would not allow his soldiery to become individual plunderers, but insisted that the booty should be equally divided. In the beginning he possessed few horsemen, but he rapidly produced a squadron of cavalry as soon as he became convinced of their usefulness. His readiness to accept advice as to the defence of Medina proved the salvation of the city. Under him the military prowess of Islam had ample scope, for he gave his leaders complete freedom of action; the result was visible in the supreme fighting quality of Ali, Omar, and Hamza, while the chances of achieving glory under his banner were the moving motives of the conversion of Khalid and Abbas. He subdued internecine warfare, and by a bold stroke united the warrior instincts of Arabia against external foes, laying upon them the sanction of religion and the promise of eternal happiness.

Though unskilled in the mechanism of knowledge—he could neither read nor write—he has left his mark upon the literature of his age and the years succeeding him. The Kuran was the sum of his inspiration, the expression in poetic and visionary language of his beliefs and ideals. He found the medium prepared. The Arabs had long previously evolved a poetry of their own which lived not in written words, but in their traditional songs. Mahomet's first flush of inspiration, which waned before the heaviness of his later tasks, is the cumulation of that wild and fervid art with the breath of the desert urgent within it.

The Kuran was never written down during his lifetime, but was collected into a jumble of fragments, "gathered together from date-leaves and tablets of white stone, and from the breasts of men," by Zeid in the first troublous years of the Caliphate. We have inevitably lost much of its original fire, and its effect is weakened by any translation into the unsuitable medium of modern speech. But that it is a valuable contribution to the literature of its country cannot be doubted, especially in the earlier portions, before Mahomet's love of harangue and the necessity of some vehicle by which to make his political dictates known had transformed its style into the bald reiterative medley of its later pages.

Through it all runs the fire of his genius; in the later suras it is the reflection of his energy that looks out from the pages; the flame itself has now lighted his actions and inspired his dreams of conquest. The Kuran is the best revelation of Mahomet himself that posterity possesses, imperfect as was the manner of its handing down to the modern world. It shows us both the beauty and strength of his personality and his cruelty, evasions, magnanimities, and lusts. More than all, the passionate zeal beating through it makes clear the secret of his sustained endeavours through discouragement and defeat until his triumph dawned.

To those outside the sphere of his magnetism, Mahomet seems urged on by a power beyond himself and scarcely within his control. His gifts bear intimate relation to the particular phase in the task of creating a religion and a political entity that was uppermost at the moment.

In Mecca he is poet and visionary, the man who speaks with angels and has seen Gabriel and Israfil, "whose heart-strings are a lute, and who has the sweetest voice of all God's creatures." He penetrates in fancy to the innermost Holy Place and beholds the God of battles, even feels his touch, icy-cold upon his shoulder, and returns with the glow of that immortal intercourse upon him. It sustains him in defeat and danger, and by the power of it he converts a few in Medina and flees thither to complete his task. In Medina he becomes a watchful leader, and still inspired by heavenly visitants, he produces order out of chaos and guards his power from numberless assaults.

In attempting to explain his achievements, when allowance is made for all those factors which gave him help, we are compelled to do homage to the strength of his personality. Neither in his revelations through the Kuran nor in the traditions of him is his secret to be found. He lived outside himself, and his actions are the standard of his accomplishments. He found Arabia the prey of warring tribes, without leader, without laws, without religion, save an idolatry obstinate but creatively dead, and he took the existing elements, wrought into them his own convictions, quickened them with the fire of his zeal, and created an embryo with effective laws, fitting social and religious institutions, but greater than all these, with the enthusiasm for an idea that led his followers to prayer and conquest. The Kuran, tradition, the later histories, all minister to that personality which informed the Muslim, so that they swept through the land like flame, impelled not only by religious zeal, but also by the memory of their leader's struggles and victories, and of his journey before them on the perilous path of warfare to the Paradise promised to the Faithful.

CPSIA information can be obtained
at www.ICGtesting.com
Printed in the USA
LVOW04s0956010516
486170LV00044B/684/P